Gender Equality?

Series Editor: Cara Acred

Volume 293

Independence Educational Publishers

First published by Independence Educational Publishers

The Studio, High Green

Great Shelford

Cambridge CB22 5EG

England

Copyright

Photocopy licence

ISBN-13: 9781861687296

Printed in Great Britain

Zenith Print Group

Contents

Introduction

Gender Equality? is Volume 293 in the *ISSUES* series. The aim of the series is to offer current, diverse information about important issues in our world, from a UK perspective.

ABOUT GENDER EQUALITY?

Is equality between men and women still an issue in today's society? Despite being closer than ever to achieving balance between the sexes, the answer is "yes". Women are still more likely to be victims of domestic violence, there are still concerns surrounding the 'gender pay gap' and men remain the traditional 'breadwinner' of the household. This book explores the stereotypes surrounding gender, considers how society is changing and looks at the myriad inequalities between men and women.

OUR SOURCES

Titles in the *ISSUES* series are designed to function as educational resource books, providing a balanced overview of a specific subject.

The information in our books is comprised of facts, articles and opinions from many different sources, including:

⇨ Newspaper reports and opinion pieces

⇨ Website factsheets

⇨ Magazine and journal articles

⇨ Statistics and surveys

⇨ Government reports

⇨ Literature from special interest groups

A NOTE ON CRITICAL EVALUATION

Because the information reprinted here is from a number of different sources, readers should bear in mind the origin of the text and whether the source is likely to have a particular bias when presenting information (or when conducting their research). It is hoped that, as you read about the many aspects of the issues explored in this book, you will critically evaluate the information presented.

It is important that you decide whether you are being presented with facts or opinions. Does the writer give a biased or unbiased report? If an opinion is being expressed, do you agree with the writer? Is there potential bias to the 'facts' or statistics behind an article?

ASSIGNMENTS

In the back of this book, you will find a selection of assignments designed to help you engage with the articles you have been reading and to explore your own opinions. Some tasks will take longer than others and there is a mixture of design, writing and research-based activities that you can complete alone or in a group.

FURTHER RESEARCH

At the end of each article we have listed its source and a website that you can visit if you would like to conduct your own research. Please remember to critically evaluate any sources that you consult and consider whether the information you are viewing is accurate and unbiased.

Useful weblinks

www.actionaid.org.uk

www.theconversation.com

www.edenred.co.uk

www.equalityhumanrights.com

www.equalpayportal.co.uk

www.girlguiding.org.uk

www.theguardian.com

www.huffingtonpost.co.uk

www.heraldscotland.com

www.inside-man.co.uk

www.mintel.com

www.modernfatherhood.org

www.natcen.ac.uk

www.newstatesman.com

www.soschildrensvillages.org.uk

www.telegraph.co.uk

touchstoneblog.org.uk

www.womankind.org.uk

www.worldbank.org

www.yougov.co.uk

Have we achieved gender equality?

In 2014, we are closer than ever to achieving equality between men and women. Worldwide, more and more girls are in education, more women occupy positions of power, and more women are in work. But with so many definitions, it can be hard to establish just how far along the road to equality we have travelled. In this article, we celebrate the successes and review the next steps on the path to achieving gender equality globally.

By Jamie Goodland

A legal matter

Changes at the policy level

Here in the UK, women gained the right to vote in 1928. For many of us, this moment represents a key milestone on the journey to gender equality. However, it was not until 1979 that the world took concerted measures to end discrimination against women. That year, the UN passed a convention known as CEDAW: the Convention on the Elimination of All Forms of Discrimination against Women.

CEDAW was the first international agreement stating women's right to be free from discrimination. It also established how this right would be protected in all those countries which signed up. CEDAW was accepted by 180 countries, which were then legally bound to adopt a series of measures ensuring the equality of men and women within society. This included changes to their legal systems based on the principle of gender equality, as well as ensuring freedom of access and opportunity within all aspects of public and political life.

Though CEDAW helped reduce discrimination, it was another decade and a half before women's entitlement to human rights were unequivocally and internationally recognised. Some had considered the UN's 1948 Universal Declaration of Human Rights to be ambiguous, arguing that its use of male terms made women's entitlement to human rights unclear – something that could be exploited by those who benefited from the subjugation of women.

In 1993, the UN World Conference on Human Rights took place in Vienna. In its Programme of Action, the conference urged for the first time "the full and equal enjoyment by women of all human rights". By agreeing that the pursuit of this objective should be a priority for governments and the UN as a collective, it set out a clear framework for the advancement of women's status in society.

But legality and reality are two very different worlds. The results have been mixed, and progress slow. With female equality finally enshrined in international law, what progress has been seen by women and girls around the world?

Progress in practice

Parisian trousers and enrolment overload

2013 saw a number of ground breaking episodes in the journey towards gender equality. One of the quirkier changes was the relaxation of French laws prohibiting women in Paris from wearing trousers. Bizarre as it may

sound, it contains a double-edged symbolism, much like the UN's 1993 prioritisation of women's human rights. The law highlighted the patriarchal structure underlying many of our legal and cultural systems. Its abolition marked the progress towards equality while at the same time demonstrating – in a world where many societies still penalise women for the clothes they choose to wear – how far we still have to go.

Nevertheless, big improvements have taken place in recent decades. The gender gap in education enrolment is closing all over the world, and in regions such as East Asia, the Caribbean and Latin America, secondary enrolment is narrowing as well. In 45 developing countries, girls have overtaken boys in secondary enrolment. Asian countries such as India, Nepal and Bangladesh have made massive strides forward. In Nepal in 1974, the ratio of boys to girls in primary and secondary education was 100:18. In 2009, girls overtook boys.

Success in Bangladesh

Family planning sparks big changes

Bangladesh is a particularly striking example, and education is a telling indicator. In 1973, little more than half as many girls as boys were enrolled in primary and secondary education. Four decades on, the figures for male and female enrolment are roughly equal. Much of that change has taken place since the late 1980s. Bangladesh has done much to address poverty. It has seen a relatively small amount of economic growth compared to other Asian countries such as India and China; however, human development has improved more quickly than in nearby countries with better economic growth.

Much of this is down to a focus on females. Famously, Bangladesh has succeeded in empowering women through family planning. Shortly after independence in 1971, the Bangladeshi Government introduced free birth control and set about distributing contraception and advice. In 1975, the proportion of women of childbearing age who used contraception was 8%; in 2010, it was 60%. In the same year, the national fertility rate – the average number of children produced by each woman – was 2.3. In the UK, it was 1.98.

The drop in fertility means that more people are entering adulthood than are being born. Crudely put, this means there are more jobs for those entering the employment market. This has wider economic benefits, but also gives women greater control over their own lives and more freedom to pursue their personal development. With employment higher and families smaller than in many other low-income countries, there are fewer pressures to encourage dropout. Welfare provision is also more robust than in many other developing countries, meaning better safety nets are in place to protect families fallen on hard times. Families are consequently motivated to educate their daughters because the risk of destitution is smaller.

The Government has also taken steps to get girls into education and maintain attendance. For example, in 1994, the Government introduced an incentive scheme whereby girls were awarded monthly cash handouts for staying in secondary education. Some studies suggests that the expansion of the garment industry has also motivated many girls to stay in school. Around 80% of employees in the sector are female, and the jobs on offer require literacy, numeracy and cognitive skills. Research also suggests that as garment jobs increase, a girl's likelihood to marry and have a child before the age of 18 drops. When families can see that education has real, long-lasting benefits, they are more likely to send their daughters to school.

Looking forward

Missing pieces

Despite these improvements, many gaps still persist. Since 1980, average life expectancy has been longer than women than for men. However, in many low- and

middle-income countries, women are more likely than men to die than in higher income countries. 3.9 million women under 60 die or go missing every year and, in sub-Saharan Africa, the number is growing.

Earnings and opportunities are lower for women. Women tend to earn less than men due to the nature of the work they do. Women are more likely to undertake unpaid family labour or to be exploited in the unregulated informal sector. Female farmers generally have smaller plots than their male counterparts; their crops generate a lower profit. When female entrepreneurs start businesses, they tend to run smaller firms and operate in less profitable sectors.

Even in Bangladesh, educated women tend to follow a predictable career path into the garment industry rather than pursue powerful or senior jobs traditionally occupied by men. Workers' rights are not guaranteed, and employees are often mistreated or even physically abused. The collapse of a factory – mostly staffed by women – in Dhaka in 2013 suggests that the safety of female employees is not always paramount. Women from other factories claim they have been beaten when reporting signs of structural damage to management.

What does the future hold?

With challenges like these to overcome, the journey towards gender equality is far from over. The case of Bangladesh makes this clear better than any. Here, women have simply been the vehicle for reducing poverty, and the value of their welfare a secondary consideration. Although women have benefited from improved living standards and better education, a large proportion of Bangladesh's female workforce perform menial jobs. Economic growth has not resulted in automatic parity for men and women in society.

Empowerment transcends economic equality in its simplest sense. Getting girls into school does not mean that they are equal to boys in a particular cultural setting if job opportunities remain segregated by gender. Education undeniably has an inherent

value, but it is also a stepping stone into the world of work, and for gender equality really to exist, that stone must lead to the same shore for men and women alike. In a separate item, we take a closer look at what women's empowerment really means, and how it can be achieved.

Gender inequality exists in many forms. While there is work still to be done, we should not be too ready to congratulate ourselves. We must also remain vigilant and be sure not to allow statistics to cloud the truth.

6 March 2014

⇨ The above information is reprinted with kind permission from SOS Children's Villages. Please visit www.soschildrensvillages.org.uk for further information.

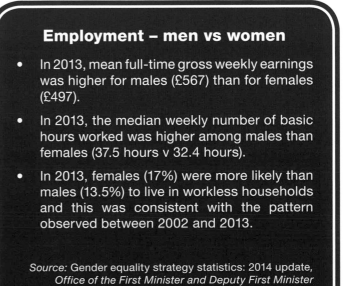

Employment – men vs women

- In 2013, mean full-time gross weekly earnings was higher for males (£567) than for females (£497).

- In 2013, the median weekly number of basic hours worked was higher among males than females (37.5 hours v 32.4 hours).

- In 2013, females (17%) were more likely than males (13.5%) to live in workless households and this was consistent with the pattern observed between 2002 and 2013.

Source: Gender equality strategy statistics: 2014 update, *Office of the First Minister and Deputy First Minister*

Emma Watson's UN gender equality campaign is an invitation to men, too

Men are welcome to join the conversation about gender equality. Let them start by listening to what women and girls have to say.

By Emma Herman

Emma Watson launched the HeForShe campaign at the UN last week and extended a "formal invitation" to men to participate in the conversation about gender equality. "Gender equality is your issue too," said the actor and UN Women goodwill ambassador. Watson's speech struck a chord with many and fanned the feminist fire that is, slowly but surely, being reignited.

The reason Watson invited men to join the conversation was that gender stereotypes also limit them. "Both men and women should feel free to be sensitive. Both men and women should feel free to be strong," she said. But while gender stereotypes can be suffocating to men too, it is women, girls and transgender people who face the lion's share of boundaries and limitations.

Let's not kid ourselves into thinking that men and women have the same stake in this drive for progress. Men wield power over women. That is the crux. And we should not ignore other dimensions: white wields power over black. Straight wields power over queer. Rich wields power over poor. Feminism is about addressing the power imbalances that limit people's opportunities to live their lives to the fullest. We need men to join the feminist pursuit of social justice because it is the right thing to do. It is a matter of human rights, not of enlightened self-interest.

At the end of her speech, Watson announced a "uniting movement", UN Women's HeForShe campaign. The initiative essentially involves a petition that men are invited to sign, committing themselves to "take action against all forms of violence and discrimination faced by women and girls". However, a movement is more than a petition. A movement is made up of people who work tirelessly to change the circumstances of their own lives as well as those of the people around them, generation after generation. The feminist movement could do with a little "uniting", but that challenge comes with the territory when you take on power in all its manifestations. Feminist activists are as diverse as the obstacles with which they grapple. A uniting movement is not worth much if it glosses over those complexities.

Besides committed people, any attempt at changing the status quo also requires ideas on how to do so beyond a viral video and a petition. Fortunately, there are people who have decades of experience in taking action against all forms of violence and discrimination faced by women and girls. They are women, girls and trans people who have been the beating heart of the feminist movement – feminist activists such as the judges and lawyers in Afghanistan who are providing women with access to legal advice and representation (Justice For All Organisation); the young domestic workers who fight exploitation and abuse in Tanzania (WoteSawa); sex workers in Thailand who show us that they deserve to be respected rather than "saved" (Empower); women in Serbia who challenge restrictive ideas about women with disabilities through art and performance (Iz Kruga Vojvodina).

These feminist activists and many thousands like them have together been leading the way for a more equal and just society for a long time. They know what strategies work and what is needed to make further progress.

That is what a movement looks like. To all those who were inspired by Watson's speech, men and women alike, I would like to say welcome to the conversation. We're thrilled to have you on board. As a first step, you're invited to listen to, and learn from, the scores of inspiring activists who make up the feminist movement. I'm sure that before long you will have lots of ideas about how you can make your pledge to "take action against all forms of violence and discrimination faced by women and girls" a tangible reality.

3 October 2014

⇨ The above information is reprinted with kind permission from The Guardian. Please visit www.theguardian.com for further information.

Men as change agents for gender equality

In 2015, UN Women will undertake a review of progress made to date against the Beijing Platform for Action, a series of commitments made by governments in 1995 to improve the lives of women and girls. In recent decades, governments, EU and UN organisations have increasingly prioritised the achievement of gender equality. This political focus coupled with the tireless commitment of civil society organisations to women's rights, has led to significant advances in the rights of women. However, inequalities, violence and discrimination against women and girls persist and will continue to persist until men and boys are engaged in the campaign for equality.

The campaign for gender equality has a long history, and each wave of feminism has seen men join the fight to improve the lives of women and girls. However such men have been in the minority and it is time for change. 2015 sees the creation of a new post-2015 global development framework, and the rights of women and girls must be placed firmly at the heart of this framework.

As stated in a recent speech by UN Goodwill Ambassador Emma Watson, the achievement of women's rights is a human rights issue and equality is everyone's business; we all have important roles to play in challenging cultural norms and stereotypes that limit us all and underpin violence against women and girls. We will not achieve equality without the engagement of men and boys, and we held this seminar to learn more about how government can work with organisations and institutions to increase the active involvement of men and boys in the gender equality campaign.

While there was disagreement in areas, particularly over how some issues are described and communicated, there was a clear shared consensus on three points:

We cannot achieve gender equality without men

Participants cited a number of ways in which men can actively promote gender equality: by taking parental leave, by sharing the double shift of childcare and housework, by challenging their peers and calling out sexist behaviours where they occur – in the street, in the workplace, and online – and by speaking about the ways in which gender inequality limits the opportunities of boys and men also.

Men will also benefit from gender equality

Men have a great deal to gain from gender equality. Restrictive gender roles and stereotypes harm men as well as women, boys as well as girls. For real change to happen, everybody has to acknowledge and understand that better for women means better for all.

Engagement is not easy

Engaging men as change agents for gender equality is not easy. But there are many men who listen, understand, and want to play their part. We must work with men to secure their involvement in making gender equality a reality. This report discusses the three points above in greater detail and identifies some of the ways government is engaging with men and boys in the campaign for gender equality. Throughout this discussion, speakers repeatedly reinforced the importance of recognising the multiple and diverse experiences of individuals, and the impact of issues including race, sexual identity and sexual orientation, religion and socio-economic background on individual experiences.

'The privilege of invisibility'

How can we explain men's lack of engagement with gender equality? Part of the problem, suggested Michael Kimmel, is that men don't see gender equality as about them because – in the popular mind – gender=women. The 'privilege of invisibility' means that those social groups with power are able to define themselves as the norm, and to see themselves as neutral, human, undefined by issues of gender, race, disability, sexuality, etc. For instance, many white people use the term 'ethnic' to refer only to black and minority ethnic people, and the white identity is frequently underexplored and unacknowledged. Men's invisibility within the concept of gender is not an oversight but a privilege and, Kimmel argued, privilege is invisible to those who own it. So one obstacle to men's engagement with gender equality is that men don't think it's about them.

Another is that while many, if not most, men agree with the concept of gender equality, fewer actively seek to divest themselves of privilege, or to make material sacrifices in order to create social change.

Finally, the gender equality area is traditionally dominated by women and therefore it may be perceived as difficult for men to enter. This point is critical and was emphasised by a number of participants. We cannot afford to underemphasise how reluctant men are to enter feminised spaces – for reasons of fear of ridicule, fear of becoming 'tainted' by femininity, and genuine concern that it is not appropriate for them to speak out about equality. This is the result of how cultural and social spaces are gendered. If men enter the sphere of gender equality, itself traditionally categorised as a woman's space, they may be seen as feminised. Equally, many women are also ambivalent about men entering this space, resenting what they see as men's attempts to define and control it, and ridiculing or criticising the legitimacy of their views.

The lives of women and girls have seen real change in recent decades: more have access to education and training; more women are in employment including in senior decision-making roles. These changes have meant that discourses around women and girls have changed. However, while we have seen challenge to heterosexual norms of masculinity from feminist and gay communities, we have not seen a similar departure from traditional definitions of masculinity to the same extent as we see a challenge to women's roles.

In the 1970s American psychologist Robert Brannon defined the four basic rules of masculinity as:

⇨ No sissy stuff – reject all that is associated with femininity

⇨ Be a big wheel – wealth, power and status define your success as a man

⇨ Be a sturdy oak – reliable and strong in a crisis

⇨ Give 'em hell – men are associated with risk, daring and aggression.

In the main these rules still apply. They are harmful to both men and women as they encourage men to suppress emotions and feelings; measure themselves by economic success and power; engage in risky behaviour and act aggressively towards women. Furthermore, they make men vulnerable to life's setbacks, particularly those involving loss of masculine status, where their learned inner resources and outer responses do not always serve them well. As an example, Kimmel cited men who experienced unemployment or redundancy and responded with an angry blaming of women for stealing 'their' jobs. A small but extremely vocal community of men believe that any gains women have made have been at men's expense, and that this has reached the level where men are in fact the sex that experiences most discrimination and least opportunity. Kimmel suggests that these men are angry because they feel disenfranchised from male privilege: the same patriarchal ideologies that promise power to certain masculine types disempower other men. Idealised constructions of masculinity give men a false sense of entitlement and then fail to deliver on it for many.

To achieve gender equality, it was argued that we must begin by confronting men's sense of entitlement and privilege. Men must be willing to recognise and challenge their positions of power in society. But equally, we need to recognise and discuss the ways in which men are short-changed by gender inequality, and demonstrate how a more equal society will be better for them, too.

What's in it for men?

The same social structures that discriminate against women shape our expectations of men and put pressure on men and boys to act in certain ways. Boys quickly learn to suppress behaviours and emotions that are associated with femininity. Restrictive gender stereotypes and representations can contribute to educational underachievement in boys, higher suicide rates in men and a lack of encouragement for men that want to work with children or in nursing. The same narrow definitions that lead to girls growing up believing that careers in science, technology and maths are not suitable choices for them mean that boys are unlikely to think of careers in caring professions. The same stereotypes that suggest ambitious and powerful women are aggressive and unfeminine mean that boys learn quickly that they must not show weakness or vulnerability; boys don't cry. Research has demonstrated that men who work in male-dominated industries such as heavy industry frequently suffer increased health problems or become socially isolated when they retire. Therefore, many men will have much to gain through gender equality that allows for new ways of working and living for both men and women.

Personal freedom

The invisibility of men in discourses of gender means that men's understanding of what it means to be male is underexamined, certainly in comparison to how women have developed a body of thought on what it means to be female. But there is sufficient research available to claim with confidence that the masculine ideal – and the social policing of it – is exacting and often brutal and tightly restricts the range of ways in which men can express their individual personalities. Participants described, and we all recognise how, from birth, boys are expected to be active and brave, to suppress emotion, to reject practices and behaviours regarded as 'feminine'. At school, at work and on the streets, they are punished for 'weakness' and rewarded for exerting control.

Men are not, generally, encouraged to express emotions associated with vulnerability – rather they are encouraged to display strength, ambition and anger. We witness hypermasculine behaviours – on the streets, in the workplace, in the home – that are clearly harmful and destructive, but little serious consideration is given to how our culture helps to create such behaviours. Men who speak out about what a lonely, frightening place the realm of hypermasculinity can be are usually treated with derision. We cannot underestimate the social penalties exacted on men for speaking out, for refusing to conform to modern masculine codes. So one of our key actions in encouraging men's engagement, participants argued, is simply to listen – even when we do not like what we hear.

What might men want to do with increased personal freedom? What trade-offs will they be willing to make with women so that we can share power and opportunity more fairly? These are questions that participants raised that we must address to engage men and boys. It was highlighted that men's attitudes towards gender equality over their lifetime can be fluid and changing. To bring about lasting social and cultural changes we need a new model of engagement that supports men and women in talking honestly and negotiating openly, with a shared understanding and acceptance of risk – the risks of societal policing and the risks of losing what few gains we have made.

To read the rest of this report, visit: https://www.gov.uk/government/uploads/system/uploads/attachment_data/file/396933/Report_on_Men_as_Agents_for_Change_in_Gender_Equality.pdf

June 2014

⇨ The above information is reprinted with kind permission from the Government Equalities Office. Please visit www.gov.uk for further information.

The best of times, the worst of times: is gender stereotyping getting better or worse?

Concern about gender stereotyping isn't new – it has been widely discussed for at least 40 years – but there is little cultural consensus about how important it is, how widespread it is and whether it is getting better or worse. The evidence suggests that it is getting both better AND worse, that as new choices and freedoms open up in some areas, pressures and restrictions are growing in others.

 More young women and men questioning traditional gender roles

 Higher employment rates for women

 Improved education and work opportunities for women

Gender studies now a highly credible and successful field of academic study

Shared parental leave, greater childcare support, flexible working

The watched body

To be a woman today is still to be defined by your body. Cultural and social norms of femininity are located in 'appropriate' female behaviour and in an idealised body image. 'Love your body, but hate it too' is the contradictory message heard by women as they attempt to combine self-esteem with achievement of an unrealistic beauty ideal. This conflict leads to high rates of anxiety, depression, eating disorders and self-harm.

Girls and women internalise street harassment, media obsession with celebrity bodies, and the 360-degree surveillance of social media into a hyper-vigillant inner eye that leads to constant self-consciousness and the performance of the self for the external viewer.

Participants told us that while there is a mass of evidence about body image and sexualisation, it is not always robust and doesn't pay enough attention to issues such as gender, race or socio-economic status. Our understanding often falls into the chasm between the psychological tradition (which has at times a simplistic understanding of the media and how it influences us) and the media/cultural studies tradition (which is under-critical of self-report data and overplays the ability of individuals to deconstruct and critique media messages). We need to learn more about how media acts as a place where cultural pressures are both created and resisted.

Have we given up changing the world to focus on tweaking our responses to it? We put the responsibility on young women to remain impervious to the cultural messages that bombard them every day, but as a society we are all responsible for querying and challenging these messages.

27 October 2014

⇨ The above information is reprinted with kind permission from the Government Equalities Office. Please visit www.gov.uk for further information.

© Crown copyright 2015

 Proliferation of gender sterotypical marketing aimed at children

 **Gender stereotyping in social media and gaming**

 Mainstreaming of pornography

 **Persisting violence against women and girls**

 **Online misogyny and abuse**

Women still under-represented in senior management and leadership roles

 Increasing pressure and focus on personal appearance

Shared inequalities: at work and at home

THE CONVERSATION

Just as women face challenges in participating in the work domain, so men face challenges participating in the home domain.

*An Article from **The Conversation**. By Stephen S Holden, Associate Professor, Bond University*

Emma Watson in her much-discussed UN speech observed that inequalities faced by women are everyone's problem, and importantly, they are only a part of the problem.

Just as inequalities are overlooked, so too are the solutions. Annabel Crabb recently observed that career women are frequently asked about how they manage their family lives while men never are.

Her solution is deceptively simple: "I don't think the answer is to stop asking women. The answer is to start asking men."

How are you managing your home life?

This question offers more than a promise of equal treatment of working women and men. It also draws attention to the need for work at home.

Unpaid household work is estimated to be equivalent to 50% of GDP. Who does this work? Women do. At a rate almost two times that of men and even greater if they have children.

However, while women do about two-thirds of the unpaid household work, men do about two-thirds of the paid work. These ratios have changed little in the last decade, suggestive of a norm.

What little change has been observed is women entering the workforce rather than men leaving. Work at home still needs to be done leading to what Crabb dubs "The Wife Drought".

Hazards of paid work

Paid work offers attractive benefits, but it also has costs. Work is harmful to health and safety.

Men have higher rates of the work-related injuries, partly due to their job choices and higher participation.

And whether related to their greater engagement with the public sphere or not, men also experience higher rates of victimisation by crime, suicide and earlier death.

So why are men not leaving the work place simultaneously easing his own burden at work and a woman's burden at home? Well, fathers who might most qualify for this job-swap face mixed signals.

No exit from work, no entry to home

While data show there has been a marked increase in stay-at-home fathers in the US over two decades, this growth is from a small base having little impact on male participation at work.

Fathers are given little encouragement as people place less value on fathers-at-home than mothers.

Various sources suggest that men are even discouraged from engaging in activities related to children.

Charles Areni and I in our book *The Other Glass Ceiling* provide other instances: a dad shopping for his daughter's undies is deemed a security risk; a single father searching for an au pair is suspicious.

Invisible barriers

Social norms are powerful and continue to operate against both men and women. Consider the following two scenarios we presented to people in some research:

"Chris is a single parent of two, a seven-year-old boy and a three-year-old girl, and also the director of marketing for a medium-sized electronics firm. Today, Chris is scheduled to present key results from the quarterly sales report to the Board of Trustees but arrives for the meeting 15 minutes late due to having to drop the older boy at school, and the younger girl at day care. In addition to dishevelled hair, there is a noticeable stain down the left side of Chris' suit, the result of the young girl vomiting at the end of her car trip after a hurried breakfast."

"Terry is a single parent to a four-year-old, James. James spends some of his time with Terry and some with his other parent. Today, three police officers and two child-safety officers have just arrived unannounced at Terry's home. The child-safety officers indicate that specific allegations have been made that Terry has been abusing James. They insist on entering the house to interview first Terry, and then James. While the accusations have been made anonymously, it is

OFFICE OR HOME?

OFFICE STRESS
UNPAID OVERTIME
STUCK INDOORS
DEADLINES
WORK PANICS
EXCESS WORKLOADS

HOUSEWORK
PREPARING MEALS
CHILDRENS HOMEWORK
SHOPPING
SCHOOL RUN

perhaps significant to note that the separation of James' parents was acrimonious."

Our research shows that 95% of people presume that Chris in the first scenario is a woman, and 82% presume that Terry in the second is a man.

However, the gender was not stated in either scenario. It appears that we associate the failures with gender-role reversals, even if unconsciously.

Family as a social support system

For better or worse, our social systems are highly specialised with roles in the home and family remaining relatively unchanged.

Gender role specialisation is changing, but slowly. The participation by women at work and men at home are increasing as roles are apparently more negotiated than presumed.

Perhaps a limiting factor is that complete equality may be unattainable. While greater male-involvement at home could reduce the child-rearing burden faced by women, he cannot reduce a woman's burden – and privilege – of being able to bear a child (as attested to by Monty Python).

In the working domain, progress is made as we see men letting go and women stepping up. This effort can be complemented in the home domain with fathers stepping up and mothers letting go.

15 October 2015

Why we'll never achieve gender equality until fathers are at the heart of family life

By Tim Porteus, Dads Coordinator, Midlothian Sure Start

Gender equality was recently put centre-stage by First Minister Nicola Sturgeon, with a commitment to ensure that no woman faces a 'glass ceiling' that limits their ambitions.

Launched last April, the Women's Pledge aims to end the gender pay gap and enhance women's work opportunities by such measures as increasing free childcare and raising the minimum wage. And while the old boys club of Westminster now has a Tory majority, Sturgeon has made it clear that "SNP MPs at Westminster will stand up for gender equality at every turn".

It's great stuff, except that men also suffer from serious and entrenched gender inequality. I understand that after centuries of struggle for women's rights, a call to recognise that men also suffer inequality has a strong taste of irony. Yet the truth is that patriarchy can only be truly dismantled when we recognise it also discriminates against men who don't want to conform to its prescribed roles. And this is particularly so when a man becomes a dad.

As I look around at fathers in my family, fathers I work with, and indeed within myself as a father of five, I see big changes taking place. More and more dads are putting their children at the heart of their priorities in ways that were unthinkable when I was wee. This is not just about rejecting sexist stereotyping of women's role in society, but also rejecting the prescriptions of their own role and identity as men. I would call it a simmering gender revolution.

Society is built around the assumption that childcare is mainly women's responsibility, and the fact women remain mostly responsible for childcare is largely the reason for the continuing gender wage gap despite decades of equal pay legislation. It is also a central reason for pay inequality and the 'glass ceiling' on women's work opportunities.

When parents work, what happens if a child is sick at school? Who takes the children to and from school? Who makes their tea, puts them to bed, gets them ready for school, washes their clothes, baths them, organises their activities, takes them to the play park? Well, likely it will be the mum and consequently her childcare commitments will affect her relationship to work, as well as hobbies and leisure time activities. That is not equality.

Real gender equality will never be won until men step up as dads. This doesn't just mean helping out now and then. It means a revolutionary redefinition of a man's role in family life, and in society as a whole. It means men engaging in a relationship with their children that defines them as equally responsible and equally involved with their children's wellbeing and upbringing. This necessarily would mean men redefining their relationship to the world of work as well.

And here is the good news: many dads are doing this already, and discovering that work, status, income, even football is less important than being dad. They are changing nappies, taking real responsibility, bonding and developing powerful attached relationships with their sons and daughters. Many are going further, structuring their lives around their children and families, rather than the other way round. They are defying the traditional expectations of their role as men.

But here is the irony: these dads hit the same discriminatory barriers that mums are so familiar with. There is a 'glass ceiling' which limits their role as parents, and their time with their children. It's the other side of the patriarchal coin: women look after the kids, men earn the money.

Society still actively and subtly promotes these gendered roles. Some maternity services are delivered as if the father-to-be were a bystander: "Make the sandwiches, put petrol in the car and do as you're told," one midwife half-jokingly told me at a parenting class in response to my question of fathers' role in labour.

Limited and unequal rights to time off work to bond and care for their baby means that health visitors rarely see dads, baby massage classes or Bookbug sessions are mum-orientated and dominated.

Playgroups and parents' events are attended mostly by mums and by the time a child reaches school age, dad has been moulded into the expected role as breadwinner, with weekends for a bit of time with the kids.

This glass ceiling, which is rarely mentioned by politicians, is reinforced by institutional bias. Many schools are satisfied with mothers' contact details, assuming fathers will get to know about important dates and events – which isn't always the case, especially when parents no longer live together. The result is a sidelining of a dad's role, reinforcing the idea that the natural order for family relationships involves dad as an optional add-on parent, rather than one of two equals in the shared parenting of their children.

But let's not kid ourselves. For millennia, most men were happy to define their masculinity this way because it gave them advantage and power. Today, many men realise that this mind-set has excluded them from their children's

childhood – and they want to be part of it; a big part.

These men are redefining masculinity. Take Crawford Goodwin, who lives in Penicuik and is full-time carer for his young granddaughter. "When my daughter was growing up I missed so much of it," he tells me. "I was at work all the time, but that's the way it was then. Now, seeing my granddaughter grow and develop I realise just what I missed with my own daughter." Goodwin is a 'man's man'. He loves his sport and good banter with the lads. But he's also a nurturing, hands-on full-time single parent for his grandchild, and loving it.

One father I worked with decided the only way to be the dad he wanted to be was to give up his job. "I had just one week's paternity leave, then had to work extra to make up for the loss of my wife's earnings. I was missing the most meaningful thing in my life: my daughter. My boss was completely inflexible. When I said I would like more flexible hours to have more time with my daughter, she said I had a wife at home to do that."

So he gave up his job and got a part-time one. But the financial sacrifice was only part of the story. "What I found hardest to cope with," he tells me, "was the torrent of judgemental comments, even from some family and friends, to the effect that I was a bad father for giving up my job, because they said it was my responsibility to bring in a wage."

But he adds: "I don't think my daughter notices that we buy less stuff. But I'm sure she does notice I'm with her most mornings, and look after her and play with her every day. And I'll still be looking for something flexible so I can be regularly at the school gates at home time."

Many single dads are quietly making the same sacrifices as mothers for their children, and doing just as good a job at parenting. As Mark, single dad of two sons, puts it: "When you have to do it then you just get on with it, for your kids' sake."

These dads don't want accolades; they just want it to be seen as normal. Women have been structuring their work life around their children's needs since the beginning of civilisation and nobody steps back in surprise to say "what a good mum" because of it. It's seen as normal.

It should be seen as normal for a dad to do this as well. The fact it isn't considered normal has allowed dads to get off the childcare hook and head for work or the pub. Many still do, and many of us think we have done our bit by doing a few dishes or buying a microwavable meal on the way home from work then telling a bedtime story. As I say, the revolution is brewing, but is yet to come to the boil. However, those fathers who don't want to get off the hook need to be encouraged and supported. With five children, I am well aware of the difficulties in work-life balance, but in the end we have to make our own priorities.

Sadly the political discourse on gender equality seems to be stuck on a perspective of the 1970s. It's as if the politicians haven't noticed the revolution brewing in fatherhood or recognised its potential role in breaking down broader gender inequality.

But like the suffragettes 100 years ago, dads are organising themselves and challenging gender inequality through action. Organisations such as Dads Rock are part of the grassroots social change in fatherhood. Set up by two Edinburgh fathers who couldn't find any playgroups for dads in the Edinburgh area, it provides a space for fathers to meet with their children.

Another example is Dynamic Dads run by Midlothian Sure Start. This provides a supportive space for fathers to spend quality time with their children. Part of the appeal is the opportunity to meet other dads because isolation is a key problem when a man is looking after the children. I experienced this myself, and found the dads' playgroup run by Dadswork invaluable.

Women are part of this change too. Michelle Davidson, who has run the parent education services at NHS Lothian, has pioneered dads2b courses in partnership with Sure Start, in which expectant dads are offered a four-week course to prepare them for their impending fatherhood. The course sees dads as equal partners in a shared parenting journey. Despite limited funding, the take-up and feedback have been excellent. "It gave me the confidence to know I am capable," says one participant.

The recent shared parental leave legislation, which came into effect last April, has been heralded as a major step forward. Parents can now decide to share the 52 weeks maternity leave and 39 weeks of statutory pay. Sounds good, but it falls far short because there is no part designated for fathers. If a dad wants more time with his baby he has to take leave from the mother, and she must be willing to give it to him. Consequently, predicted take-up is very low. In Sweden, the designated two months' paid paternal leave for fathers is almost universally taken up, significantly boosting gender equality in that country.

Here in the UK, real progress won't be achieved until it becomes culturally unacceptable for men to avoid taking on their share. Designated paternal leave would do precisely that. If we are serious about equal rights for men and women then we need a cultural transformation in which fatherhood and motherhood are seen as two sides of the same coin, of equal status and with the same expectations and responsibilities.

Exclusion and negative stereotyping of fathers must end, and their involvement has to be actively promoted through policies such as 'dad-proofing': which means organisations taking steps to ensure fathers feel included rather than excluded. Such a policy is operated at Prestonpans Infant School, where my daughter is in Primary 1, to ensure conscious efforts are made to incorporate a father's dimension in everyday teaching.

As I write. I am looking forward to tomorrow as the school is being opened to dads for a Father's Day message from their own children. My daughter is lucky enough to have a male teacher who has shown her that nurture and empathy is not gender-specific at school.

Fathers who are separated from their children's mother can be at the sharp end of gender inequality, since the default position within courts and social services is still that children should be with the mother. When there is conflict between parents, dads often have to prove themselves as worthy of the right even to have access.

This exclusion is damaging our children. All the evidence shows that having a loving nurturing dad in a child's life is in the child's interest.

So since today is Father's Day let us say loud and clear that discrimination against dads must no longer be ignored by politicians and policy-makers. Next year has been designated Year Of The Dad, and as part of it there will be the creation of a 'Father's Pledge', which is it is hoped will involve service providers, dads and employers getting together to find ways to dad-proof society. Let all who believe in equality support this and make it a partner to the 'Women's Pledge', because they are, as I have said, two sides of the same coin.

If a woman can be first minister then a man can nurture and care for his children. Ending gender inequality is possible, but only if we recognise that women are not the only victims of it.

21 June 2015

⇨ The above information is reprinted with kind permission from *Herald Scotland*. Please visit www.heraldscotland.com for further information.

We shouldn't fight for 'gender equality'. We should fight to abolish gender

Gender is flawed – no set of social scripts will ever represent the wonderful diversity and intricacy of human behaviour.

By George Gillett

'Gender equality' seems to be the go-to phrase right now. Since Emma Watson launched the HeForShe Campaign, a rush of public figures including Barack Obama, Russell Crowe and Prince Harry have pledged their support, while social media users have been similarly keen to promote the cause. Indeed, the expressed aim of achieving 'gender equality' is one which appears to have amassed almost universal backing.

But what if gender equality isn't enough? As an end-goal, it feels stunted, incomplete and short-sighted. The problems which surround gender encompass far more than a conventional inequality – our archaic belief in the concept of gender itself undermines ideals of personal freedom and liberation.

Gender is defined by the World Health Organization as "the socially constructed roles, behaviours, activities, and attributes that a given society considers appropriate for men and women". In other words, while sex refers to biological and physical characteristics, gender describes the behavioural roles that we associate with these features.

Our endorsement of the concept of gender lends itself to the creation of gender roles; personality types based on traits that are 'masculine' or 'feminine'. The effects of such limited categorisation are rapidly being realised – for instance, the effect of rigid gender roles on the wellbeing and physical health of men and women is well documented. Similarly, sexism, homophobia and body dysmorphia all result from these insidious attitudes about what makes an 'ideal' man or woman.

A number of high profile campaigns, including the HeForShe Campaign, are gradually challenging many gender-based assumptions. Likewise, many journalists and academics have called for the redefinition of words such as masculinity and femininity. These campaigns imply that by dispelling 'harmful' stereotypes we can create alternative, positive, constructions of gender.

Yet such a belief is paradoxical – the existence of gender itself is, by definition, inherently oppressive. The aspects of a gendered identity which one person deems to be positive will equally act to oppress another member of the same sex, who would be unrepresented by such a definition. In fact, the diversity of men and women means that creating a unanimously positive personality type is simply impossible. And even if such an attribute was identified, its association with a specific sex would imply that people of other identities lacked this characteristic. Not only is this concept of gender harmful, but the noxious idea that we can associate a positive set of behavioural characteristics with a physical sex is intrinsically flawed.

At this point, those who proudly endorse the notion of gender utter something along the lines of: "but… science!" And yes, some evidence does suggest that biological differences contribute to behavioural differences between the sexes. For instance, studies have shown that women score better on empathy tests, and that girls are more likely to show concern for others compared to boys. Moreover, it's unlikely that these differences result entirely from socialisation – researchers have even found distinctions in how male and female newborn babies respond to faces and mechanical objects.

Yet, even if brain differences between the sexes do exist (the evidence is extremely contentious), such findings don't legitimise the construction of an all-encompassing social 'gender'.

These studies identify quantitative differences based on numerical averages calculated from groups of men and women. It is another thing entirely to apply this crude data to individuals, who are much more intricate, complex and diverse than a statistical average could ever describe.

Worse still, by applying these statistical findings to our conversations about gender, we curtail freedom and liberation in favour of a perverse form of genetic determinism. Gender cannot healthily co-exist with a sense of personal freedom; to liberate someone within the confines of a statistical interpretation based on the body they were born into is not really liberation at all.

Others argue that many of these issues can be avoided by redefining gender as a spectrum, consisting of an array of identities. But this is still problematic – belief in a gendered spectrum still upholds the idea of one-dimensional variation between two extremes of maximal 'masculinity' and 'femininity'. Most perversely, creating an array of gender identities to pick from doesn't eliminate the apparent need for society to establish pre-determined moulds for people to draw their identity from.

What, exactly, is so scary about individuals creating their own unique identity, regardless of their physical sex? Whether obsessing over the products we buy, clothes we wear, or toilets we use, society is fixated with controlling people's behaviour based on arbitrary gendered groupings. This creates genuine turmoil for anyone who feels limited by traditional gender assumptions, but applies especially to the trans community, whose oppression is such that 41 per cent have attempted to commit suicide.

And we are all complicit in this. When questioned what we mean by describing ourselves as a man or woman, if we answer with anything other than a description of our physical genitalia (and how society treats us), we contribute to the preservation of the divisive and oppressive notion of gender.

The future, however, shows promise. In Sweden, for example, a gender-neutral pronoun has been added to the National Encyclopaedia and is commonly used by the mainstream press. Meanwhile Facebook recently adjusted their settings to cater for a wider range of gender identities, including those who reject gender constructions entirely.

Yet, despite sensationalist tabloid articles arguing otherwise, it seems that our discontentment with gender is anything but a modern phenomenon. In popular culture, we've long admired figures who have defied the constraints of gender. Perhaps society's adoration of figures such as David Bowie, Mick Jagger and Annie Lennox can be attributed in part to our neglected need to consider human beings as people – unique, engaging and diverse people – which is only truly possible when oppressive gender roles are proudly abandoned.

With each gender stereotype that is dispelled, we move a step closer towards equality and liberation. But instead of trudging along the laborious and indirect path of eliminating these stereotypes one at a time, we should be clear and proud of our aims. Indeed, the façade of 'redefining' masculinity and femininity isn't a compromise, it's a contradiction. The aim of 'gender equality' doesn't go far enough – we need to confront the very concept of gender itself.

2 October 2014

Oxford English Dictionary may include the gender neutral title 'Mx' alongside 'Mr' and 'Mrs' in new edition

By Rachel Moss

Most forms will require us to tick a box marked 'Miss', 'Mr', 'Ms' or 'Mrs', but selecting a title from these options can be problematic for some transgender people.

That's why government departments, high street banks, some universities, councils and the Royal Mail all now accept 'Mx'.

On top of that, the gender-neutral title is now being considered for inclusion in the next edition of the *Oxford English Dictionary (OED)*.

We say, about bloomin' time.

"This is an example of how the English language adapts to people's needs, with people using language in ways that suit them rather than letting language dictate identity to them," Jonathan Dent, assistant editor of *OED* told *The Sunday Times*.

"When you look at the usual drop-down options for titles, they tend to be quite formal and embrace traditional status such as the relationship between a man and wife, such as Mr and Mrs, or a profession such as Dr or even Lord. This is something new."

The news that *OED* may include Mx comes after 'hen' became the third official pronoun in Sweden.

The gender-neutral pronoun – which can be applied to objects and people who don't wish to specifically identify as male or female – was added to the Swedish Academy's official dictionary in March.

5 May 2015

Blurring gender lines in the toy aisle

By Stacy Glasgow

For my niece's birthday this year, she requested Spiderman paraphernalia. With shopping list in hand, I headed to the toy store, ever mindful of achieving Aunt of the Year status. Perusing the aisles, it occurred to me that not so many years ago I might have had to go to the 'boy' section of the store to find superhero products. Nowadays, toy stores and other retailers are starting to abandon the push to sell products to specific genders.

Industry leaders such as Amazon recently removed the 'boy' and 'girl' filters from their toy department's search page. Now, you'll find dolls in the 'Dolls' section and action figures in the 'Action Figures' section, instead of each being housed within sections labelled by those toys' presumptive target genders. Amazon's move follows in the footsteps of Toys R Us in the UK, which in 2013 partnered with a parent group in a pledge to phase out gender-specific marketing within their stores.

The imminent obsoleteness of pink and blue toy aisles is reflective of a broader societal shift toward gender equality and blurred gender lines. Most recently:

⇨ With the women's World Cup playing out this month, Nike is offering US women's soccer team jerseys in men's sizes for the first time ever.

⇨ Headquartered in New York, investment banking firm Goldman Sachs has doubled the paid paternity leave for non-primary caregivers from two weeks to four.

As Mintel predicted in the 2015 US Consumer Trend Gender Agenda, the conversation around gender is louder this year than it ever has been in the past, with people questioning traditional ideas of gender roles, rejecting the restraints of stereotypes and embracing the freedom to be themselves and do what they want.

As this overall conversation continues to grow louder, so too do the voices calling attention to how gender stereotyping can affect children. The Mintel Trend Let Kids Be Kids examines how parents who want to raise their kids as individuals are taking a more open-minded approach to child-rearing and are moving away from traditional gender stereotypes. In other words, they don't want to see their children be forced into labelled boxes – 'boy' and 'girl' – and they don't want their children's lives to be defined by all that comes with those labels.

Tiffe Fermaint, the co-founder of US-based Baby Teith – a new company that specialises in gender-neutral, eco-friendly baby and kids' clothing – summarised the opportunity this trend presents for brands in a recent statement:

"We genuinely believe that in this day and age, gender stereotypes are outdated. We want our daughter to form her own opinions on the subject and feel that she can dress any way she wishes. Instilling this notion before she forms opinions like 'Pink is just for girls' and 'I have to wear pink because I am a girl' can be an important step. We are extremely happy to see more clothing in the market that is gender-neutral. The market is changing and we hope that bigger brands take notice. This is a huge step for gender equality."

Other brands have taken similar stances in regard to children's gender labelling:

⇨ The UK's children's book publisher Ladybird announced that it will no longer brand books as 'for girls' or 'for boys' in a bid to reduce gender stereotypes. The company signed up to the Let Books be Books campaign which attempts to remove gendered labelling from books.

⇨ Yoga Joes are US-created army figurines that are doing a range of yoga poses. The maker of Yoga Joes hopes to help encourage kids, men and military veterans to give yoga a go. The figurines reflect consumers becoming more open-minded about what constitutes appropriate behaviour for men and women.

⇨ Clothing brand Lands' End bowed to public pressure and launched science-themed shirts for girls as well as boys in the US.

⇨ UK father Sam Farmer has created a range of unisex beauty and personal care products for young people.

Additional opportunity for brands lies in potential partnerships with the increasing number of kids' gender-related initiatives we've seen, such as:

⇨ Supermodel Karlie Kloss launched a partnership with the Flatiron School in New York to create a Kode with Karlie Scholarship for 20 girls aged 13–18 to teach them how to code. The programme is a two-week, full-time course where students will take an intro to a software engineering course and explore concepts in back-end software engineering. Students will also learn how to create an app using coding languages.

⇨ American photographer, Lindsay Morris, launched a project, including a book called *You Are You*, which explores the new generation of gender-creative kids. Morris began by photographing children who attended an annual long-weekend camp for gender-nonconforming children and their families. Children aged six to 12 attend with their parents and siblings and participate in typical summer camp activities – canoeing, hiking, crafts – and at the end of camp, there's a fashion show with a red carpet and runway.

Brands that place this type of message at the core of their business will win the support of parents who don't want to limit their child's development to stereotypes associated with their gender. As summed up in Mintel's 2015 Consumer Trends, "gender is not going away anytime soon, but its restrictive aspects are."

22 July 2015

⇨ The above information is reprinted with kind permission from Mintel. Please visit www.mintel.com for further information.

Ladybird drops branding books 'for boys' or 'for girls'

Much-loved publisher of books for youngsters says it does not want 'to be seen to be limiting children in any way'.

By Alison Flood

Ladybird, the iconic publisher of children's books including the classic Peter and Jane reading scheme, has vowed to remove any 'boy' or 'girl' labels from its books because it doesn't want "to be seen to be limiting children in any way".

The publisher, which is due to celebrate its centenary next year, is the latest to sign up to the Let Books Be Books campaign, which argues that labelling books with titles like *The Beautiful Girls' Book of Colouring* or *Illustrated Classics for Boys* sends the message "that certain books are off-limits for girls or for boys, and promotes limiting gender stereotypes".

Ladybird's gendered titles include 2011's *Favourite Fairy Tales for Girls* and *Favourite Stories for Boys*, the former claiming that "the mix of princesses, fairies and classic characters is perfect for little girls everywhere", and including stories such as *Cinderella* and *Sleeping Beauty*, the latter that "the lively mix of adventurous heroes, dastardly creatures and classic characters is perfect for boys everywhere", and including *Jack and the Beanstalk* and the *Three Little Pigs*.

Ladybird said that it only had six titles with "this kind of titling", and told campaigners that "following discussions, should any of the titles you mention be reprinted for the trade we will be removing this labelling".

"At Ladybird we certainly don't want to be seen to be limiting children in any way. Out of literally hundreds of titles currently in print, we actually only have the six titles you cite… so I do feel we offer a vast range for children and their parents," the publisher told campaigners, adding that its parent company, the huge Penguin Random House children's division, would also be following its new stance. "As Ladybird is part of the Penguin Random House Children's division, our commitment to avoiding gendered titles in the trade crosses all our imprints."

Campaigners believe that "a good book should be open to anyone, and children should feel free to choose books that interest them". Their petition to children's publishers has gathered thousands of signatures, as well as the support of authors from Neil Gaiman to Joanne Harris. Gaiman has said that "Books are for people. Stories are for people. Limiting that is foolish and short-sighted"; Harris that "what may seem to be a harmless marketing strategy, is, to an impressionable child, really a form of brainwashing, repeating the false message that boys are brilliant and brave, while girls are mostly just decorative". Malorie Blackman, who said that "part of reading for pleasure is letting our children and young adults choose the books they want to read for themselves", and Anne Fine adding that "it's a serious matter because it does narrow children's sense of what they're allowed to do or like, in a horrible, horrible way", are also supporters of the campaign.

Heather Crossley, Ladybird's publisher, said: "We would hate to be seen to be limiting imaginations in any way and I don't feel we do that. The signposting of 'for boys' and 'for girls' was initially to make it easier for purchasers, for example for grandparents buying gifts. A lot of publishers have done that in the past. But we feel we have titles which can be enjoyed by both genders, so it makes sense to take the labelling off... I know if a boy found his favourite title happened to be in the girls' collection, he wouldn't be too chuffed."

The publishers Miles Kelly, Chad Valley, Usborne, Parragon and Dorling Kindersley – part of Penguin – have all confirmed they will not publish any more boy or girl titles, while Waterstones has also thrown its support behind campaigners. The stationer Paperchase committed in the summer to removing its Boys Activity Pad and Girls Activity Pad from sale.

"At Miles Kelly, we value and produce high-quality content that's suitable for both boys and girls, and agree that both genders should simply be encouraged to read, whether they like vampire stories, dinosaur facts or classic fairytales! We think kids should be able to choose freely what interests them, so we have removed gendered messages from four of our books. We have no plans to publish any new gendered titles in the UK,"

said Amanda Askew, marketing director at Miles Kelly.

Two publishers, Buster Books and Igloo Books, have yet to respond to Let Books Be Books' calls to remove their gendered titles. Buster declined to comment further on Thursday, having told *The Guardian* in March that "when you have a colouring book which is specifically for a boy or a girl, it sells three times as many copies as one without the sexual categorisation"; Igloo Books did not respond to a request for comment.

Tricia Lowther from Let Books Be Books said: "We are delighted that Ladybird has joined the ranks of publishers who have agreed to Let Books Be Books and that this commitment extends to the Penguin Random House Children's division too. It's great that they have recognised these titles can be limiting for children. Hopefully those few remaining publishers of gendered titles will realise that children deserve more than gender stereotypes."

The campaigners are now turning their sights on Christmas, and on urging those shopping for presents

to avoid taking the gendered route. "It's always better to buy based on what a child is interested in rather than by assumptions of what they might like based on their gender. There's no good reason for children's books to be packaged as for boys or girls – don't let marketers limit children's horizons by saying otherwise. A good book is for anyone," said Lowther, pointing shoppers towards "inclusive" retailers such as the online book retailer Letterbox Library, and the News from Nowhere Bookshop in Liverpool, and asking the public to nominate more using the hashtag #Toymark on Twitter.

20 November 2015

⇨ The above information is reprinted with kind permission from *The Guardian*. Please visit www.guardian.com for further information.

We must stop indoctrinating boys in feminist ideology

Feminist organisations, backed by government policy, are teaching young boys at school to feel guilty and ashamed of their gender, writes Dan Bell.

On Wednesday, the *Daily Mail* reported that a school in Oxford has become the first to introduce "Good Lad" workshops, in which boys are singled out for sessions that teach them about "the scale of sexual harassment and violence aimed at female students" and how they must stand up for women's rights.

The workshops are the latest in a mushrooming series of initiatives in which ideologically-driven activists are being invited into schools, driven by the belief that boys need to be re-educated to prevent them from becoming a threat to women.

In November last year, *The Times* reported on a programme in London Schools in which two American women, one a former sex crime prosecutor, "re-programme teenage boys' sexual manners so they are fit for a feminist world".

According to the report, they start the class by asserting that "misogyny is on the rise", before going on to "describe real-life sex crimes that have happened to teenagers in this area with brutal accuracy". The article concludes – approvingly – that by the end of the session, the boys are "scarred for life".

In context of the chasm between boys' and girls' educational attainment and a rising male suicide rate that is now nearly four times that of women's, why are schools deciding that when it comes to talking about gender, what boys need most is an extra dose of guilt and shame?

Another organisation, A Call to Men UK, also goes into schools, stating on its website: "A CALL TO MEN UK believes that preventing violence against women and girls is primarily the responsibility of men. We re-educate through trainings (sic), workshops, presentations, school projects and community initiatives."

And yet another, the Great Men Value Women project, frames its mission as about helping young men, but it's also driven by the belief that young men need to be re-educated as feminists – not just for their own good,

but for women's too. On the section of their website listing the organisation's values, their final point simply states: "Feminism: This says it all", with a link to a video of TED X talk entitled: "We Should All Be Feminists".

Really? Who says so? Most importantly though, since when was it acceptable to impose ideology on school children? And for that matter, would we ever dare to suggest school girls ought to be taught that Great Women Value Men?

By all means, let's teach children about healthy relationships, but that's not really what these campaigns are about. Instead there is an overwhelming emphasis on imposing an ideological worldview that first and foremost sees young men as potential abusers and perpetrators, while routinely ignoring and minimising the very real threat of violence, both physical and sexual, that boys and young men face themselves.

You'd never know it from the rhetoric, but a man – and particularly a young man – is around twice as likely to be a victim of violent crime as a woman. And it's not just drunken street violence either. A 2009 NSPCC report into domestic violence in teenage relationships, showed teenage boys suffer comparable rates of violence from their girlfriends as do teenage girls from their boyfriends.

In the same year another report, this time by Childline, found that of the children who called to report sexual abuse, a total of 8,457 were girls (64%) and 4,780 were boys (36%). The charity also found boys were more likely to say they had been sexually abused by a woman

(1,722 cases) than by a man (1,651).

At the time, Childline founder Esther Rantzen, said the charity had specifically reached out to boys, because they were convinced the higher number of calls they had been receiving from girls "could not be explained by the fact that boys encountered fewer problems than girls".

Imagine what it must it be like as a young man who has been beaten or sexually abused, possibly by a woman, to then be forced to attend a workshop that tells him that simply because he's a young man, he should hang his head in shame as a potential abuser?

Neither are these activist interventions just the preserve of a few radical head teachers: they in fact reflect official government policy.

In March, the Government announced the introduction of new consent classes for children aged as young as 11. The plans were launched on International Women's Day and the PSHE guidelines repeatedly state they are primarily part of the Government's *A Call to End Violence Against Women and Girls* strategy.

According to a 'Fact Sheet' published by one of the guidelines' key contributors, a top priority for the lessons is "challenging notions of male sexual entitlement" and the lessons should be seen "in the context of a society in which gender inequality is the norm… and girls and young women are subjected to high levels of harassment, abuse and violence – overwhelmingly from men and boys they know".

Apparently, in the eyes of the Government, schoolboys don't so much see girls as their friends and peers, but as potential prey.

And the indoctrination doesn't stop when a boy leaves school, it continues when he gets to university too – the 'Good Lad' workshops in Oxford, are in fact a spin-off from compulsory consent classes for new male students that are now springing up across UK universities.

What impact must all this be having on boys and young men, who are themselves at one of the most vulnerable stages of their lives? Last year, insideMAN published findings of a focus group of young male students, which gave a disturbing glimpse into the ideological classroom climate faced by boys, this time told by young men themselves.

They told us that when it came to expressing any view that contradicted feminist orthodoxy, they were shouted at and publicly humiliated. They said their motives routinely came under immediate suspicion simply on account of their gender. And they said they wanted to be protected against fundamentalism by

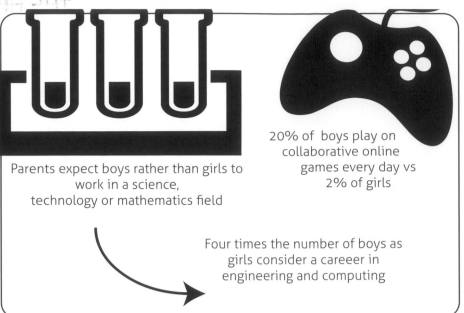

Parents expect boys rather than girls to work in a science, technology or mathematics field

20% of boys play on collaborative online games every day vs 2% of girls

Four times the number of boys as girls consider a careeer in engineering and computing

prominent and leading figures in the campaign for gender equality.

If boys like these are already coming under attack in A-Level English classes, what might they expect in a PSHE lesson that – as one of the new suggested lesson plans propose – puts them through a "conscience alley", in which they are asked to take on the role of a potential rapist, then walk between their classmates who tell them what they think of their behaviour?

In 2001, novelist and feminist icon Doris Lessing made a shocking assessment of what she had seen while visiting a school classroom.

She told the Edinburgh Book Festival, "I was in a class of nine- and ten-year-olds, girls and boys, and this young woman was telling these kids that the reason for wars was the innately violent nature of men.

"You could see the little girls, fat with complacency and conceit while the little boys sat there crumpled, apologising for their existence, thinking this was going to be the pattern of their lives."

Lessing expressed deep concern that what she had witnessed was just a glimpse of an increasingly pervasive culture of toxic feminism in schools that was weighing down boys with a collective sense of guilt and shame.

She had every right to be worried. It seems there is now a drive to make shame and guilt a formal part of boys' education.

20 July 2015

⇨ The above information is reprinted with kind permission from *The Telegraph*. Please visit www.telegraph.co.uk for further information.

Our ancient ancestors may have known more about gender than we do

An article from **The Conversation.**

By Karina Croucher, Lecturer in Archaeology, University of Bradford

THE CONVERSATION

A recent advert by sanitary product manufacturer Always asks us to think harder about the term "like a girl" by asking young adults and teenagers to run, throw or fight "like a girl". Without thinking, regardless of gender, they run with flailed arms, fight doggy paddle style, and pretend to throw pathetically. When asked the same question, young girls run like themselves – active running, real throwing, and packing punches you wouldn't want to be on the receiving end of.

While the advert is ultimately about marketing and designed to improve brand image, it nevertheless asks us to consider when the phrase "like a girl" becomes an insult, asks us why there's such a noticeable drop in confidence as girls hit puberty. And it asks us why being "like a girl" is demeaning. Such

attitudes undoubtedly contribute to the perpetual inequalities we know are still faced around gender equity, whether in education, employment, or wages.

What does this have to do with archaeology? The past is frequently used, consciously and unconsciously, to reinforce what we consider to be normal. And the idea of fixed genders with their associated roles and identities is especially true of this. Archaeological material has frequently been used to reinforce these ideas about gender – and it's not far from this to "like a girl".

But considering archaeological evidence from another angle, it becomes apparent that our expectations of gender roles can be problematic. In ancient terms, our gender divides are far from

universal. It is not the experience everywhere that gender falls neatly into binary categories of male or female; that is, into being either male or female, with nothing in between. In fact, the evidence suggests that much of what we perceive as core components of our identity were not significant categorising factors in the past. Rather, we see ambiguities in identities repeatedly represented in the material culture from archaeological sites.

It's often the case that the material is difficult to define or pigeonhole. Take, for instance, the stone monoliths from the site of Göbekli Tepe in Southeast Turkey. These shrine areas containing huge monoliths were constructed around 6,000 years or more before Stonehenge. The great pillar structures have traditionally been interpreted as representing male, phallic imagery.

I would argue that this is by no means the case. As well as being impressive in their scale, many have been carved with additional features such as arms, hands and loincloths or belts. They are clearly ambiguous in their nature, neither human nor stone. We know the sculptors clearly had the skills to create naturalistic carvings, but they deliberately chose to make these different, ambiguous, crossing between one type of being and another. This says less about gender, and more about the fluid conception these ancestors had about the universe.

Similar issues are frequently encountered. In clay figurines, for example. Clear gender categories are found in some material, but there are others which are difficult to define. From the Neolithic of the Middle East, my region/period of study, the vast majority of human figurines don't portray either

male or female features. Many figurines actually combine male and female characteristics into single figurines, or appear either male or female when viewed from different angles. Our categories of male and female just don't work when analysing them. This is something which is now being recognised by archaeologists – our understanding is blinkered by our own perspectives of gender categorisation, and this will have determined our analysis to some extent.

Because of this, male imagery is traditionally thought to indicate themes of dominance and females are ascribed to domestic spheres. But the archaeology of the Late Neolithic of the Middle East – the roots of our own civilisation – doesn't suggest much evidence for very differential labour roles or treatment. As has been demonstrated by a team of experts at Çatalhöyük, women and men spent comparable periods of time within the house, ate the same diets, engaged in comparable tasks (leaving skeletal markers on bones) and were buried in the same ways.

And at a site called Domuztepe, a feature called the Death Pit was found which contained the remains of around 40 people who had been specially treated after death and the focus of funerary feasts. No observable difference in the treatment of males or females was discernible. And this pattern is repeated in various mortuary assemblages, such as in the phenomena of plastering skulls dating to a couple of millennia earlier. This was a practice previously thought to be unique to males, but it's now recognised that comparable numbers of men and women were treated this way.

So there are numerous examples of apparent gender equity, as well as examples of more ambiguous third gender representation. Most skeletal collections contain a proportion which are not easy to categorise as male or female. This raises issues for the historical basis of our understandings of gender, gender roles and identities.

As recent news stories demonstrate, there is growing recognition of the problematic nature of strictly binary gender categories, including the acceptance of third gender pupils in schools in India, or on changes in law in Germany to include a third gender category on birth certificates.

But many countries still insist on pigeonholing children into narrow identity confines. Perhaps history and archaeology could be used to support rather than undermine minorities, for once.

We need to challenge what it is to be "like a girl", where these ideas came from and how they have proliferated. If our gender categories and the identities they promote are problematic, then biases and inequality based on these differences become even more flawed. We need to talk about all these issues, and particularly interrogate the well-worn narratives that are used to support these ideas. Archaeology is no bad place to start.

13 August 2014

⇨ The above information is reprinted with kind permission from *The Conversation*. Please visit www.theconversation. com for further information.

Women in the UK Regular Forces, 1 July 2014

	Total		Officers		Other ranks	
	Number	%	Number	%	Number	%
Total armed forces	157,490		27,760		129,730	
of which women	15,780	10.0	3,530	12.7	12,250	9.4
Royal Navy	33,080		6,780		26,300	
of which women	3,010	9.1	680	10.0	2,330	8.9
Army	89,480		13,190		76,290	
of which women	7,920	8.9	1,550	11.8	6,370	8.3
RAF	34,940		7,800		27,140	
of which women	4,850	13.9	1,300	16.7	3,550	13.1

Source: UK Armed Forces Quarterly Manning Report, DASA

Gender equality in the world of work matters

Executive summary from Gender at Work, A companion to the World Development Report on Jobs.

Jobs can bring gains for women, their families, businesses and communities

Jobs boost self-esteem and pull families out of poverty. Yet gender disparities persist in the world of work. Closing these gaps, while working to stimulate job creation more broadly, is a prerequisite for ending extreme poverty and boosting shared prosperity.

Gender equality in the world of work is a win-win on many fronts

A large and growing body of evidence demonstrates both the business and the development case. Booz & Company estimates that raising female employment to male levels could have a direct impact on GDP, increasing it by 34 per cent in Egypt, 12 per cent in the United Arab Emirates, ten per cent in South Africa, and nine per cent in Japan, taking into account losses in economy-wide labour productivity that could occur as new workers entered the labour force. Yet almost half of women's productive potential globally is unutilized, compared to 22 percent of men's, according to the International Labour Organization. In places where women's paid work has increased, as in Latin America and the Caribbean, gains have made significant contributions to overall poverty reduction.

Both the World Development Report 2013 on Jobs (WDR 2013) and the World Development Report 2012 on Gender Equality and Development (WDR 2012) provide valuable and complementary frameworks to help policy makers advance gender equality in the world of work

The WDR 2013 approach helps us to understand how and when promoting gender equality in the world of work adds significant development value. The WDR 2012, meanwhile, offers an important framework for diagnosing and addressing gender-specific constraints. An important link between the two WDRs is the notion of agency – women's ability to make choices they value and to act on those choices. Jobs can increase women's agency by expanding their life choices and their capacity to better support their families and more actively participate in communities and societies. Conversely, significant constraints on agency pose major barriers to women's work and help explain the persistence of gender gaps.

Following the WDR 2013, 'jobs' are broadly defined to include various forms of wage and non-wage work, formal and informal

Informal work is the largest source of employment throughout Africa, Asia and the Middle East, and working women are more likely than working men to be self-employed or farming. The jobs that are best for women's economic empowerment – and development goals more broadly – depend on country-specific jobs challenges.

Where do we stand?

Gender equality in the world of work is multidimensional

Broadly, key dimensions include labour force participation, employment, firm and farming characteristics, earnings and job quality. The last is the most difficult to measure and varies by context. However, full-time wage employment is a strong predictor of

subjective wellbeing, and jobs that provide higher earnings, benefits, rights, and opportunities for skills development are more likely to expand women's agency.

On virtually every global measure, women are more economically excluded than men

Trends suggest that women's labour force participation (ages 15–64) worldwide over the last two decades has stagnated, declining from 57 to 55 per cent globally. Participation is as low as 25 per cent in the Middle East and North Africa. Globally, Gallup estimates that men are nearly twice as likely as women to have full-time jobs – and, in South Asia, they are more than three times as likely.

Gender gaps are evident among farmers, entrepreneurs and employees alike

Because of gender-specific constraints, female farmers tend to have lower output per unit of land and are less likely to be active in commercial farming than men. In the Central Highlands of Ethiopia, the value of output per hectare of female-headed households has been estimated to be 35 per cent lower than that of male-headed households, a disparity stemming mainly from unequal access to productive inputs. Female entrepreneurs typically operate smaller firms and in less profitable sectors. In Latin America

and the Caribbean, half of established businesses owned by women have no employees, compared to 38 percent of businesses owned by men. Female employees are more likely to work in temporary and part-time jobs, are less likely to be promoted, and are concentrated in occupations and sectors with lower barriers to entry. Women and girls also do the vast majority of unpaid care and housework.

Women generally earn less than men

ILO analysis of 83 countries shows that women in paid work earn on average between ten and 30 per cent less than men. Gaps are particularly acute in the Middle East and North Africa, but also persist in high-income OECD countries. Gender sorting into different jobs, industries, and firm types explains much of the pay gap. Throughout the world, women are concentrated in less-productive jobs and run enterprises in less-productive sectors, with fewer opportunities for business scale-up or career advancement. The latest Grant Thornton *International Business Report* indicates that the share of women in senior management roles globally is only 24 per cent. Across developing countries, 18 per cent of non-agricultural self-employed males work in business-oriented services, compared to only five per cent of females; women are more heavily concentrated in retail services, often in the informal sector.

Overlapping disadvantages and gender equality at work

Gender-smart jobs strategies need to identify and address multiple deprivations and constraints that underlie gender inequality in the world of work

The *WDR 2012* provides a valuable framework for understanding the challenges. It highlights key outcome areas – agency, endowments, and economic opportunities – and underscores the fact that disparities are driven by multiple constraints that arise in formal and informal institutions, markets and households. The constraints are most severe among women who face other disadvantages, such as being a member of an ethnic minority, having a disability, or being poor.

Social norms are a key factor underlying deprivations and constraints throughout the lifecycle

Norms affect women's work by dictating the way they spend their time and undervaluing their potential. Housework, child-rearing and elderly care are often considered primarily women's responsibility. Further, nearly four in ten people globally (close to one-half in developing countries) agree that, when jobs are scarce, men should have more right to jobs than women. Research shows that women are frequently disadvantaged by gender biases in performance and hiring evaluations.

Jobs can increase women's agency, but a lack of agency also restricts women's job opportunities

In most developing countries, women have fewer choices in fundamental areas of day-to-day life, including their own movements, sexual and reproductive health decisions, ability to use household assets, and whether and when to go to school, work or participate in other economic-related activities. Further, a large proportion of women in the world lack freedom from violence. The World Health Organization estimates that more

than 35 per cent of women have experienced gender-based violence. Without addressing these critical constraints on agency, women cannot take full advantage of potential economic opportunities.

Inequalities in endowments and assets contribute to gaps in the world of work

While there has been important progress globally, in some countries fundamental deprivations persist. In 2010–12, female-to-male enrolment ratios for primary school were less than 90 per cent in 16 countries, mainly in Africa, and some 57 million primary school age children were not enrolled. Many women lack access to land and financial capital. Other deep-seated differences also persist. For example, young women and men often follow different educational streams and develop differences in aspirations and skills that underlie occupational segregations later in life. A wider account of productive inputs shows women disadvantaged in areas such as access to financial services, technology, training, information, and social networks.

Legal discrimination is a remarkably common barrier to women's work

Of 143 economies, 128 had at least one legal differentiation in 2013. These barriers include restricting women's ability to access institutions (such as obtaining an ID card or conducting official transactions), own or use property, build credit or get a job. In 15 countries, women still require their husbands' consent to work. In many economies, especially in the Middle East and North Africa, women face the cumulative effects of multiple legal constraints.

Published in 2013

⇨ World Bank. 2014. *Gender at Work, A Companion to the World Development Report on Jobs*. Washington, DC.

Equal pay statistics

In this article, EqualPayPortal looks at official sources of information on the gender pay gap within the UK and across Europe. We also look at what information there is on the number and outcome of equal pay cases filed with the Employment Tribunal.

European data on the gender pay gap

Inequality in pay between men and women remains high on the European agenda. The unadjusted gender pay gap is an important indicator used within the European Employment Strategy to monitor imbalances in wages between men and women. Eurostat, the European Commission equivalent of the UK's Office for National Statistics, publishes a summary of *Gender Pay Gap Statistics* which includes links to other sites with relevance to the gender pay gap.

United Kingdom data on the gender pay gap

Some words of warning: always check whether the data refers to the United Kingdom, or to Britain. Some official data sources also provide information specifically on Scotland and Wales, but this is often inadequate. Also check the time frame within which the data is collected, as this may vary from one source to another, meaning that any comparisons have to be treated with caution.

Methodology

At the whole economy level the gender pay gap is calculated from data drawn from the *Annual Survey of Hours and Earnings* (the *Annual Survey*), which is carried out by the Office for National Statistics (the ONS). The Annual Survey is based on a one per cent sample of employee jobs, drawn from Her Majesty's Revenue and Customs Pay As You Earn records. The *Annual Survey* collects information on the levels, distribution and make-up of earnings and hours paid. Results are produced by gender and by various industrial, occupational and geographic breakdowns, as well as by public and private sectors and age groups. In the absence of an annual report on the gender pay gap in the UK (as, for example, that produced by Belgium) the *Annual Survey* is the key official source of information on the gender pay gap in the UK.

Various methods can be used to measure the earnings of women relative to men. The ONS headline estimates of the gender pay gap are for hourly earnings excluding overtime. The ONS uses median, rather than mean, earnings because the median is not affected by extreme values, such as changes in the earnings of small numbers of very high earners. However, as those on very high earnings are predominantly male, and those on very low earnings predominantly female, the mean is an important measure of women's experience of labour market disadvantage as compared to men, and one which allows international comparisons to be made.

To get a full picture of women's earnings relative to men's it is important to read the annual statistical bulletin in its entirety, and not just the section on the gender pay gap.

Equal pay for equal work

Although median and mean hourly pay excluding overtime provide useful comparisons of men's and women's earnings, they do not reveal differences in rates of pay for comparable jobs, and it is rates of pay for comparable jobs which are the focus of the equal pay legislation.

While the Office for National Statistics rightly states that this is because such measures do not allow for the different employment characteristics of men and women, such as the proportion of men and

Only 27% of women on low pay say they always have enough money to cover their household living costs

58% of women on low pay have enough money some or most weeks

15% of women on low pay rarely or never have enough money to cover their house-hold living costs

Source: Life for women on low pay: research by Survation for the Fawcett Society

women in different occupations and their length of time in jobs, the most important reason why the comparisons do not reveal differences in rates of pay for comparable jobs is that in the absence of a national framework for job evaluation (as exists, for example, in some Eastern European countries), a national survey cannot take account of job demands.

For these reasons the headline figures for the gender pay gap should not be treated as an indicator of whether women are receiving equal pay for equal work.

Up to date information on the gender pay gap

On November 19th 2014 the ONS released provisional results for the *Annual Survey of Hours and Earnings*. These show that in the year to April 2014, average earnings for full-time employees increased by 0.1%. The gender pay gap decreased from 10.0% to 9.4%.

Men working full-time earned £558 per week in April 2014 compared with £462 for women, with both seeing small increases compared to 2013 (0.3% and 0.6%, respectively), and there were 236,000 jobs that paid less than the minimum wage.

The report goes into the gender pay gap in some detail:

⇨ The gap for all employees (full-time and part-time) was the lowest on record at 19.1%, down from 19.8% in 2013. The gap has also decreased in the long-term, from 27.5% in 1997.

⇨ For part-time employees, the higher rate of pay for women than men results in a 'negative' gender pay gap. Although the trend is more volatile than for full-time employees, there is evidence that the gap has widened in the long-term. It has, however, remained relatively stable in recent years, standing at 5.5% in April 2014.

⇨ The gap is relatively small up to, and including, the 30-39 age group (with the exception of the 16–17 age group). In fact, the gap is negative for the 22–29 and 30–39 age groups, meaning that women earn on average more than men. Thereafter, there is a relatively large positive gap.

⇨ At the 90th percentile (higher earners), the gap is the lowest since the series began (18.3%), although over time this has remained largely consistent, fluctuating around 20%. For lower earners the gap has narrowed over the long term, to 5.9% in April 2014.

⇨ In April 2014, the gender pay gap for the private sector decreased from 19.2% to 17.5%, the lowest since the series began in 1997. The gap in the private sector has consistently been greater than for the public sector.

⇨ The gap in the public sector increased from 9.5% to 11%, although the report notes that this has been relatively stable over the longer term, fluctuating around 10% since 2003.

The report points out that the composition of the public and private sectors changes from year to year, and this will influence the figures presented. For example, in a given sector, creation of jobs in higher paying occupations with a high proportion of female employees would act to reduce the gap. The report omits to mention that clusters of higher paying jobs

10% of women on low pay have obtained a loan from a payday lender in the last 12 months.

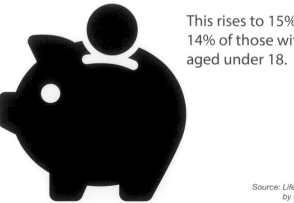

This rises to 15% of under 35s and 14% of those with a child aged under 18.

Source: Life for women on low pay: research by Survation for the Fawcett Society

Over one in five of the low-paid women polled by Survation had degree-level qualifications...

37% of these women feel overqualified and over-skilled for their job

Among those who feel this way, one of the top three reasons is: caring for children (16%)

Source: Life for women on low pay: research by Survation for the Fawcett Society

with a high proportion of female employees are found only in the public sector, where the pay gap is in fact widening.

For further information from the Office of National Statistics

For further information on the *Annual Survey* contact: James Tucker, Annual Survey of Hours and Earnings earnings@ons.gsi.gov.uk

The gender pay gap over time

In March 2014 the DCMS, using ONS data sources, carried out an analysis of how the gender pay gap has changed over time. A breakdown of the gender pay gap by age, occupation and income percentile is included. The analysis does not look at ethnicity, nor at region, but it is reasonable to suppose that the high concentrations of both men and women from ethnic minorities in particular regions and occupations and in part-time working, must have an impact on the findings and on the conclusions that can be drawn from them.

Key points:

⇨ The gender pay gap for all staff in the UK in 2013 was 19.7 per cent, as measured by hourly earnings for all employees. This was marginally higher than in 2012, when the gender pay gap was 19.6 per cent. However, the pay gap has decreased markedly over the longer term. This paper looks at changes in the gender pay gap over this longer period by: age; occupation; and for high/low earners.

⇨ The gender pay gap, and how it has changed over time, varies for the different age groups. In 2013, the gender pay gap was lowest for those in the youngest age groups. It then increases up to the 40 to 49-year-old age group, before falling for the older age bands. Between 1997 and 2013, the gender pay gap has, in general, narrowed for all age bands up to and including 40- to 49-year-olds. For the oldest age groups the pay gap has stayed fairly static since 2005.

⇨ Median earnings rose faster between 1997 and 2013 for women between 30 and 39 than for any other age group. This has coincided with the pay gap for this age group decreasing by more than any other.

⇨ The gender pay gap within different groups of occupations varies considerably, and has changed in different ways for occupations between 1997 and 2013: The pay gap has consistently been high for those in the skilled trades (plumbers, electricians, etc.), and for managers and directors. The pay gap has been consistently lower than the national average for professional and associate professional occupations. With increased attendance at universities, there have been more people (and proportionately more women) entering these occupational groups.

⇨ The gender pay gap across high and low earners also varies. In 2013 the gender pay gap was lowest for those in the 10th percentile of earnings (the value which 10% of the population earn less than). The pay gap has also decreased by the most for this group between 1997 and 2013. The gender pay gap has decreased in a similar manner for those between the 40th and 80th percentiles of earnings. However, the gender pay gap for those earning the most has not decreased by as much as the other groups between 1997 and 2013. This shows that the gap between the highest earning males and females is not narrowing at the same rate as the rest of the economy.

17 September 2015

⇨ The above information is reprinted with kind permission from EqualPayPortal. Please visit www.equalpayportal.co.uk for further information.

Decline of male breadwinner family across Europe

There has been a decline in male breadwinner families across Europe, according to new findings from NatCen Social Research, the Institute of Education's Thomas Coram Research Unit and the University of East Anglia (UEA).

Two-parent families where only the father works have become a minority in many European countries and make up only around a fifth (22%) of families in the UK, according to analysis of data from the EU Labour Force Survey between 2001 and 2011.

⇨ The biggest falls in male breadwinner families were in Spain down to 28% of families in 2011 from close to half (49%) in 2001, Greece 36% down from 46% and The Netherlands 17% down from 27%.

⇨ Levels in Germany (25%), France (22%) and the UK (22%) were more stable but are among the lowest in Europe.

The research, part of the ESRC-funded Modern Fatherhood project, will be discussed today (3 July) at the Modern Fatherhood conference – Fathers, Work and Families in 21st Century Britain – at The University of London's Institute of Education.

Dr Sara Connolly, a Reader in Personnel Economics at UEA's Norwich Business School, said: "We are seeing not only a greater level of equality in economic provisioning between parents but also a growth in new working models involving more part-time and other flexible forms of employment."

Work and family life

Further research being presented at the conference will look at conflict between UK fathers' working and home lives and how this varies across Europe.

Of the eight countries looked at in the European Social Survey, UK fathers reported the highest levels of conflict between paid work and family life.

⇨ 35% of UK fathers said they always or often worry about work problems when not working; 17% said this never happens.

⇨ 37% of UK fathers said they are always or often too tired after work to enjoy the things they would like to do at home; 8% said this never happens.

⇨ However, only 10% of UK fathers said that family responsibilities prevent them from giving the time they should to their job always or often; 26% said it never happens.

⇨ Fathers in the UK and Greece were most likely to say that work interfered negatively in their family life, while fathers in The Netherlands were least likely.

The research also shows that it is those fathers who worked longer hours who were most likely to report conflict between their working and home lives.

Dr Svetlana Speight, NatCen Social Research said "This research shows that in the UK many fathers allow their job to undermine their family life. It suggests that there are lessons we can learn from countries like the Netherlands where fathers appear to have a better work-life balance."

The impact of work on family life is of particular interest in the context of analysis of the EU Labour Force Survey being presented at the conference, which shows significant changes in UK fathers' working arrangements between 2001 and 2011.

The research shows fathers working a shorter working week and a significant decline in the proportion of fathers working evenings, nights or weekends.

⇨ The usual working week of fathers working full-time in couple households has fallen from 47 to 45 hours per week.

⇨ The proportion of fathers who say they never work evenings rose from 33% to 52%, those never working nights rose from 66% to 76% and never working at the weekend rose from 26% to 45%.

⇨ In 2011, fathers were also much less likely than in 2001 to be working shifts – a fall from 24 to 21%.

Professor Margaret O'Brien, Director, Thomas Coram Research Unit said: "Nearly one third of British fathers still usually work over 48 hours a week and a tenth over 60 hours a week. If the Coalition government is really serious about being family friendly it should sign up to the EU Working Time Directive which will take pressure off British families and allow parents the choice of sharing work hours between them in a more balanced and modern way."

3 July 2014

⇨ The above information is reprinted with kind permission from NatCen Social Research, UCL Institute of Education and University of East Anglia. Please visit www.natcen.ac.uk or www.modernfatherhood.org for further information.

Women and the workplace: how roles have changed

Over the last century, gender roles have changed dramatically – not just in the home and in society generally, but in the workplace as well. No longer are women expected to endure a life of domestic drudgery; in some countries at least, their right to go out and earn a wage is now almost universally acknowledged. While there is still some way to go before we can say that we have true gender equality at work, it's nevertheless worth noting just how much progress has been made over the last 100 years.

Women at work: the present day

In the present day, women are far more visible both in work and across public life than they were in previous decades. Women occupy prominent roles in business, politics and the media alike. Even so, there's still a lot of work to be done – according to the Fawcett Society, the gender pay gap is 14.2%, with women effectively working for free from 9 November until the end of the year in comparison to their male co-workers.

So why is it that women are still denied equal opportunities and equal representation at work? One key reason is that age-old gender biases refuse to die. Many women are denied top jobs for fear that they may choose to have children. Sir Alan Sugar infamously admitted that he would be reluctant to appoint women to senior roles for this reason. More women are delaying having children to pursue career goals. The Office for National Statistics reported in 2013 that the average age of all mothers had risen to 30 for the first time on record.

It took many years for women to get to this point – and it's worth reflecting on just what previous generations of women were faced with.

Women's work in wartime

Up to the outbreak of the First World War in 1915, female employment outside the home was relatively marginal. Many working-class British women were consigned to domestic servitude, leaving them at the whim of their employers and forced to endure frequently dismal conditions including a real lack of personal autonomy. At the start of the war, many of these women found themselves out of work as their middle-class employers started to trim back their domestic expenses. Female unemployment rose noticeably as a result.

However, it soon occurred to the Government that with thousands of men heading off to Europe to fight, the munitions industries were short of labour. Over the next four years, 1.6 million women were added to the workforce. Some – the 'munitionettes' – worked in the munitions industries, taken into government control in 1915. Other sectors which saw a boom in female employment included the postal service, civilian manufacturing, public transport and the civil service.

Women were again called up for war work as the Second World War intensified. To begin with, only single women were required to work outside the home, though by the middle of 1943 80 per cent of married women were also employed for war work. Some 640,000 women even joined the armed forces despite not being required to. Wartime nurseries were provided by the Government to provide accessible childcare, although they were closed down soon after the war and it was again assumed families would be catered for by male breadwinners. The gains made by women were harder to reverse than they had been after the First World War, however.

What can be done?

Germany has offered one example as to how we might tackle underrepresentation of women in the boardroom. Legislation passed in March requires large firms to allocate at least 30 per cent of places on their board to women by 2016. Another 3,500 medium-sized firms will be required to draw up their own quotas. However, positive discrimination provokes instinctive hostility not just among a lot of men but also some women who fear their achievements won't be taken seriously in their own right.

The increasing self-confidence and assertiveness of women generally bodes well for those seeking equality at work. More women are attending university than men, and they also tend to emerge from higher education with more qualifications. This ought to stand them in good stead when they come to seek work, in spite of the continuing challenges they face. And the fact that more women are being appointed to top roles should encourage others in their own efforts to advance up the ladder.

What's essential for equality at work is that everyone has the opportunity to flourish and develop. Generations of women have struggled for the right to do precisely that. That struggle isn't yet over, but it continues to bear fruit. Those who continue to resist workplace equality don't just risk putting themselves on the wrong side of history – they risk missing out on valuable talent and experience as well.

12 November 2015

⇨ The above information is reprinted with kind permission from Edenred. Please visit www.edenred.co.uk for further information.

Why are we paying men who work part-time less than part-time women?

Glen Poole examines why part-time men are earning less than part-time women on average.

In August 2014, we revealed that the biggest gender pay gap for people under 40 is experienced by men who work part-time and we looked at the selective use of statistics that keeps this fact hidden from the general public.

This week we decided to take a closer look at the part-time gender pay gap and discovered that in every age bracket, the average man who works part time will earn less than the average woman who works full time per hour.

There are currently around two million men working part time in the UK. Here we provide five little known facts about the part-time gender pay gaps that impact men based on figures from the Department of Culture Media and Sport and the Annual Survey of Hours and Earnings (ASHE).

1. Men who work part-time earn less than part-time women

According to the Government's provisional figures for 2013, the average median pay for men who work part-time across all age groups is £7.90 per hour, compared with £8.40 for women.

This equates to a 5.4% gender pay gap in favour of women. Using the same calculation for full-time workers, the average median pay for men who work full-time across all age groups is £13.73 per hour, compared with £12.15 for women (a gender pay gap of 11.5%).

	Women	Men	Pay gap
Full-time workers average hourly pay	£12.15	£13.75	11.5%
Part-time workers average hourly pay	£8.40	£7.90	5.4%

Put simply, men who work part-time earn less per hour on average than women who work part-time.

2. The part-time pay penalty is 58% bigger for men than women

When you look at the gaps between full-time pay and part-time pay for men and women, it's clear that the gap for men is considerably larger.

Men who work part-time experience a pay gap of 42.1% compared to men who work full time, while women who work part-time experience a gap of 26.7%.

	Full-time	Part-time	Pay gap
Men's average hourly pay	£13.73	£7.90	42.1%
Women's average hourly pay	£12.15	£8.40	26.7%
Differential	11.5%	5.5%	57.7%

Put simply, men who work part time will fall further behind their full-time peers, in terms of their earnings, than women who work part time.

3. The part-time pay gap is bigger for men who work in the private sector

When we compare the public and private sector we find that the majority of part-time workers are found in the private sector. This is particularly noticeable for men who are four times more likely to be working part-time in the private sector than the public sector.

The average median pay for the 1.2 million men who work part-time in the private sector across all age groups is £7.13 per hour, compared with £7.33 for the 2.9 million women who work part-time in the private sector, a gender pay gap of 2.7%.

There are also 291,000 men working part time in the public sector, accounting for 14.2% of the part-time workforce. They earn 17.5% more than the 1.8 million who work part-time in the public sector on average. This is presumably because of the large number of women working part-time in lower paid, public sector jobs such as childcare and social care.

There are a further 200,000 men and 582,000 women who work part time and not classified as working in either the public or the private sector.

	Men	Women	Pay gap
Private sector part-time hourly pay	£7.13	£7.33	2.9%
Public sector part-time hourly pay	£12.70	£10.48	17.5%
Unclassified	£10.76	£9.26	13.9%

Put simply, most part-time men work in the private sector and they earn 2.9% less per hour than their female colleagues.

4. The part-time pay gap for men is found across multiple occupations

The tendency for men to earn less per hour when they work part time is found across nearly all occupations. The only exception is the professions where both men and women who work part-time earn more than colleagues of the same sex who are working full time.

One of the key cause of the gender pay gap is the fact that more women work part time and end up earning less than the majority of male colleagues who are more likely to work full time. This trend is repeated in reverse with men who work part time earning less per hour than female colleagues who work full time.

The biggest gender pay gaps for part-time men (compared with full-time women) are found at management level (8.4%) and amongst administrative staff (11.2%).

Job types	Part-time men	Part-time women	Pay gap
Managerial	£15.06	£16.44	8.4%
Professional	£21.64	£18.49	17%
Technical	£12.59	£13.53	6.9%
Administrative	£8.75	£9.85	11.2%
Skilled trades	£7.50	£7.97	5.9%
Leisure and care	£8.03	£8.25	2.7%
Sales and customer service	£6.85	£7.14	4.1%
Process, plant and machine operatives	£7.55	£7.61	0.8%
Elementary occupations	£6.48	£6.69	3.2%

Put simply, men who work part-time earn less than male and female colleagues who work full time in all occupations except for the professions.

5. The part-time pay gap is biggest for men in their thirties

Men who work part-time earn 5.4% less than part-time women on average, based on median hourly pay. However, the part-time gender pay gap varies with age. For part-time men, for example, the biggest gap occurs in 30–39 age group where the gender pay gap is 7.8%.

Another notable difference is that the part-time male workforce continues to increase its average earning power throughout their career, rising from a pay of £6.50 per hour in the teen years to £9.86 per hour at 60+.

Part-time female workers follow a different earnings trajectory rising more rapidly from £6.40 per hour in the teen years to a peak of £9.40 in the 30-39 age range. After 40, part-time women continue to earn more than the under-30s, but earn increasingly less each decade, falling back to £8.65 per hour at 60+.

This is presumably due the seniority of part-time positions that men over 40 take on when compared with women.

Age	Male part-time	Female part-time	Pay gap
All ages	£7.95	£8.40	5.4%
18–21	£6.50	£6.40	1.5%
22–29	£7.40	£7.47	0.9%
30–39	£8.67	£9.40	7.8%
40–49	£9.70	£9.00	7.2%
50–59	£9.81	£8.97	8.6%
60+	£9.86	£8.65	12.3%

Put simply, men who work part-time earn 5.4% less per hour than part-time women on average, but men's part-time earnings improve slowly with age for men.

4 September 2014

⇨ The above information is reprinted with kind permission from Inside Man. Please visit www.inside-man.co.uk for further information.

Close the gap! The cost of inequality in women's work

Extract from the report by Action Aid.

By Kasia Staszewska

Today, hundreds of millions of women will collect firewood and water for their families, cook and clean, take care of the elderly, the young and the sick; all the while scratching a living from the poorest paid and most precarious jobs. Women's labour – in and outside the home – is vital to sustainable development, and for the wellbeing of society. Without the subsidy it provides, the world economy would not function. Yet it is undervalued and for the most part invisible.

To reveal the scale of the crisis, ActionAid has calculated the economic value of addressing gender inequality in work in developing countries. Our findings show that women in developing countries could be US$9 trillion better off if their pay and access to paid work were equal to that of men. This huge price tag illustrates the magnitude of the injustice and represents a vast mine of untapped potential for poor women to improve their own lives, and those of their families. And these costs are not only to women's finances; women's economic inequality limits their life choices too – such as their sexual and reproductive health and rights – leaving them vulnerable to violence and other forms of discrimination and exploitation.

But gender inequality in work not only has consequences for women; it carries major costs for all, including businesses and the wider economy. In 2012 the International Labour Organization (ILO) estimated that globally an additional US$1.6 trillion in output could be generated by reducing the gap in employment between women and men.[1] Ensuring that women's work, both in and

outside the home, is valued and rewarded fairly is a key factor in fighting poverty and driving prosperity for all.

Recognition is growing worldwide that our economic system needs profound reform. There is also increasing understanding that economic growth alone is not going to lead to gender equality, alleviate poverty and reduce inequality for all. A few governments have taken bold steps to address gender inequality in work, while some progressive businesses have shown greater understanding that giving decent work opportunities[2] to women goes hand in hand with sustainable business and economic returns. The challenge remains to spread this vision from the champions to the mainstream.

Women's economic inequality is not inevitable. Exploitation of women's work prevails because of the unjust politics that shape our economy, and because it is rooted in and further drives wider gender discrimination in society. Governments, businesses and international institutions all have the power to create the conditions that are needed to give women in developing countries the chances that they deserve in and at work.

Women and work – education is no guarantee

Most people would expect that significant progress in increasing the number of girls in schools over the past two decades[3] would improve the life chances and opportunities for women. However, the consistently low participation rates of young women in the job market prove that the knowledge and skills that they have acquired are systematically ignored.

Our research shows that in 2013 in low-income countries, more than twice as many women with a secondary education were unemployed than men with the same education.[4]

Disparities vary from region to region and country to country reflecting the scale of the challenge young women

1   The International Labour Organization (2012) *Global employment trends for women* http://ilo.org/wcmsp5/groups/public/---dgreports/---dcomm/documents/publication/wcms_195447.pdf p.14

2   After the ILO ActionAid identifies four aspects of decent work agenda: creating jobs, guaranteeing rights at work, social protection and social dialogue, with gender equality as a cross-cutting objective. See: http://www.ilo.org/global/about-the-ilo/ decent-work-agenda/lang--en/index.htm Accessed 12/2014

3   United Nations (2014) *The Millennium Development Goals Report 2014* http://www.un.org/millenniumgoals/2014%20MDG%20report/MDG%202014%20English%20web.pdf

4   Economists Without Borders (2014) *Gender Discrimination and Unemployment, report for ActionAid.* See http://datatopics.worldbank.org/Gender/topic/education which shows that in most regions of the world female secondary school enrolment is lower than male secondary school enrolment, therefore we can assume that the over-representation of educated women among the unemployed does not simply reflect a greater number of women educated to a secondary level than men in wider society

face in the search for jobs. For instance, in the Middle East and North Africa almost 60% of unemployed women hold advanced degrees, while the same statistic for men is at 20%.[5]

Double standards: women paid little and always less than men

Entering employment does not automatically lead to empowerment and equality for women. Many women and men, especially in developing countries simply do not earn a living wage – in other words, enough to have a decent standard of living and meet their own and their families' basic needs.[6]

What's more, when women are paid for a job, they earn on average between 10% to 30% less than men for work of equal value.[7] The ILO estimates that at the current rate of progress it will take 75 years to make the principle of 'equal pay for equal work' a reality for women and men.[8]

Women's exploitation in the labour market is further compounded by their disproportionate share of unpaid care responsibilities (such as child rearing, domestic chores, and caring for the sick and elderly), which effectively means that women are subsidising the economy with free and often invisible work.

Unpaid care responsibilities narrow women's choices in the type of job they get, often condemning them to informal or low-paid employment and dramatically swelling their hours of work overall. So it is unsurprising that women's wages everywhere lag far behind those of men. In developing countries, according to ActionAid's calculations, this has created a gender wage gap equivalent to some US$2 trillion in women's earnings, or as much as the worth of India's entire economy.[9]

2 January 2015

⇨ The above information is reprinted with kind permission from ActionAid. Please visit www.actionaid.org.uk for further information or, to read the whole report, visit http://www.actionaid.org.uk/ sites/default/files/publications/ w o m e n s _ r i g h t s _ o n - l i n e _ version_2.1.pdf.

© *ActionAid 2015*

5   Ibid

6   Unlike the minimum wage, the living wage is an informal benchmark, not a legally enforceable minimum level of pay. It is based on the amount an individual needs to earn to cover the basic costs of living for themselves and their family. According to the ILO Conventions 95 and 131: "Wages and benefits paid for a standard working week should meet at least legal or industry minimum wage standards and always be sufficient to meet basic needs of workers and their families and to provide discretionary income." The call for living wage has received widespread support from civil society organisations, trade unions and some political parties, but limited endorsement by employers.

7   The World Bank Group (2014) *Gender at Work: A Companion to the World Development Report on Jobs* http://www.worldbank.org/content/dam/Worldbank/ Event/Gender/GenderAtWork_web2.pdf p.2

8   The International Labour Organization (2011) Report of the director general: A new era of social justice, International Labour Conference, 100th Session, Geneva 2011, http://www.ilo.org/wcmsp5/ groups/public/@ed_norm/@relconf/documents/ meetingdocument/wcms_155656.pdf p.11

9   See: http://timesofindia.indiatimes.com/business/ india-business/India-set-to-become-2-trillion-economy- this-year/articleshow/44881279.cms Accessed 12/2014

On average women spend at least twice as much time on household work than men and four times as much time on childcare.

Many women don't earn a living wage and receive 10% to 30% less pay than men for work of equal value.

Women face discrimination in corridors of power and are denied rights to collection organisation. In January 2015 only 13 finance ministers worldwide, and on average one in five parliamentarians, were women.

Out of 143 economies 90% have at least one law restricting economic equality for women.

Women make up 60% of the world's working poor, they are denied access to decent work and experience exploitative conditions at work.

Women's rights are human rights

Communications Volunteer Rosalind Bygott says it's time the world recognised that women's rights are human rights...

Sixty-four years ago today, the UN proclaimed 10 December as Human Rights Day to "bring the Universal Declaration of Human Rights to attention as the common standard of achievement for all peoples and all nations". It marks the end of 16 Days of Activism, which aims to raise awareness of violence against women and girls as a human rights issue at the local, national, regional and international levels.

As the United Nations Secretary General, Ban Ki Moon, said: "Violence against women continues to persist as one of the most heinous, systematic and prevalent human rights abuses in the world. It is a threat to all women, and an obstacle to all our efforts for development, peace and gender equality in all societies. Violence against women is always a violation of human rights; it is always a crime; and it is always unacceptable. Let us take this issue with the deadly seriousness that it deserves."

In her speech at the United Nations Fourth World Conference on Women in Beijing in 1995, Hillary Clinton coined the phrase "women's rights are human rights". For decades women activists have campaigned for legal frameworks and practical action to protect and promote their rights.

Womankind's partners are carrying out vital work in communities to secure the rights of women and support women to live free from violence. But a lack of funding is preventing them from having long-term impact. Violence against women and girls is one of the most widespread violations of human rights, with one in three women worldwide experiencing violence in her lifetime. Violence denies women and girls the right to a life free from abuse and subjects them to inhuman and degrading treatment.

At the start of 16 Days of Activism, on the International Day for the Elimination of Violence against Women (25 November), Womankind launched a research paper *Prevention is possible* on the role of women's rights organisations in ending violence against women and girls in Ethiopia, Ghana and Zambia. Drawing on the experiences of our partners, it highlights the importance of tackling the underlying causes of violence and the vital role of women's rights organisations in working to address it.

The research identifies a number of factors that enable positive changes in attitudes and behaviours across the three countries. These include: individual awareness of the negative consequences of violence against women and girls, community members modelling new non-violent behaviours, commitment to change by community leaders, public condemnation of violence against women and women's empowerment and solidarity. With funding and support, women's rights organisations working on the ground can continue to work with local communities to shift negative attitudes and behaviours towards women.

We need to remember that – despite how far we've come with recognising the need for universal human rights – we are still not where we should be. In the three countries studied in the research, almost half of women aged 18–49 reported experiencing physical violence since age 15. While so many women face such gross violations, we are still very far from a world where human rights are for everyone.

⇨ The above information is reprinted with kind permission from Woman Kind. Please visit www.womankind.org.uk for further information.

© Woman Kind 2015

Girls' Attitudes Survey 2014

Executive summary from the Girlguiding survey.

The *Girls' Attitudes Survey* this year shows that girls and young women continue to experience significant challenges in their lives, many of them because of their gender. The daily pressures and discrimination they face, as our new evidence shows, can have a serious impact on their well-being and affect how they behave and participate in different spheres of their lives. Many of those surveyed voice very serious concerns, and share disturbing experiences, on issues such as bullying, violence against women and girls, sex and relationships education, the representation of women in the media, body image and women's political participation. Too often, the data shows that girls and young women are told not to take these experiences seriously or are encouraged to normalise discrimination they face.

However, this year we also document how girls and young women think some of these persistent and emerging challenges could be tackled. They overwhelmingly support the vibrant campaigns currently in the headlines, the Everyday Sexism project and the No More Page Three campaign among them. The findings suggest that despite the challenges they face, girls are aware of their right to equality, know that they should expect better, have ideas for how to get there and are speaking out to demand change. We include many of their voices in the report.

Wellbeing and mental health

The findings on wellbeing and mental health are shocking and very worrying. Three in four girls aged 11 to 21 know girls their age who self-harm (76%) or suffer from depression (73%), and two in three know someone with an eating disorder (66%). Bullying is reported as a major problem too. Significant numbers say that they know girls their age who have experienced racist bullying (42%), homophobic bullying (40%) and bullying about a disability (31%). Although many of these issues sadly also affect boys, this data indicates the toll these pressures take on the well-being of girls and young women specifically. Girls say that more education on mental health would be one way of helping them.

Violence against women and girls

The findings on girls' and young women's experiences of gendered violence are also distressing. Three in five of those aged 13 to 21 (59%) have experienced sexual harassment at school, college or work in the last year. Despite the seriousness of the problem, 61% of girls of secondary-school age (11 to 16 years) say teachers or staff sometimes or always dismiss sexual harassment as just a bit of banter – 'boys mucking around'. Girls themselves overwhelmingly support campaigns that aim to change attitudes, and this report includes some of their ideas for tackling violence against them.

Relationships and sex

The majority of girls and young women aged 11 to 21 think that all schools should have to teach about sex and relationships (74%). Girls and young women report that the Sex and Relationships Education (SRE) they get at school isn't good enough – with only 39% of those aged 13 to 21 saying the provision they had was good. They want to see SRE cover a wider range of issues relevant to their lives today, and some of their suggestions are included in this report.

Everyday sexism

Overall, 85% of those aged 11 to 21 say they experience sexism in some aspect of their life. Girls report that the main arenas for this are the media (see 'Women in the media' for details), social media, schools and colleges, and public places. The negative impact of this experience is clear – girls feel angry, less confident, embarrassed or degraded, and less safe. Yet many girls clearly expect better and also report their appetite for fighting back, with the majority supporting campaigns that challenge sexism, and several saying that their experiences make them more determined to speak out.

Women in the media

Girls and young women are critical of the ways in which the media portrays women, and report seeing widespread media sexism. Three

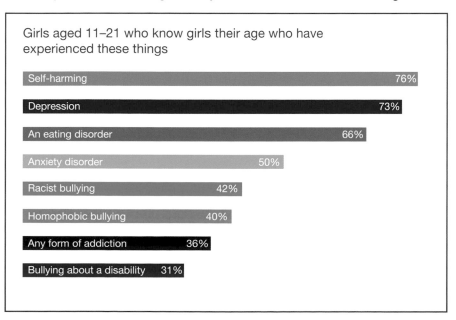

Girls aged 11–21 who know girls their age who have experienced these things

Self-harming	76%
Depression	73%
An eating disorder	66%
Anxiety disorder	50%
Racist bullying	42%
Homophobic bullying	40%
Any form of addiction	36%
Bullying about a disability	31%

quarters of those aged 11 to 21, and 48% of younger girls (seven to 10), think there are too many images of naked or nearly naked women in the media. They don't like the way women are disrespected in music videos (57%), and the majority are critical of victim – blaming in cases of sexual violence (58%). Instead, they want to see a greater diversity of women represented, and believe that both media organisations (89%) and the Government (85%) have a role to play in making sure that the media represents all women fairly.

Appearance pressures

As in previous years, the findings show that girls and young women are feeling pressure to conform to body-image ideals and that this affects their behaviour and well-being. They feel pressure to be 'thin' and to go on diets, and to look more like celebrities they see in the media. This results in almost half of 11- to 21-year-olds sometimes feeling ashamed of the way they look (45%), and two in five (39%) not taking part in fun activities because they are self-conscious about their appearance. Lessons on self-esteem and more media responsibility in showing realistic images of women are among solutions from girls.

Careers

It is clear that careers advice is largely failing girls and young women currently. Almost equal numbers of girls and young women rate their experience of careers advice as bad (26%) as they do good (29%). A shortage of up-to-date information about what types of jobs are available and gender bias in the provision of advice contribute to this dissatisfaction. We asked girls and young women for their views on why the gender gap among those studying science, technology, engineering and maths (STEM) subjects persists, and we report some of their ideas for what could help close that gap.

Political participation

Though the data shows that only a minority of girls and young women are interested in politics

Girls aged 13–21 who have experienced any of the following at school/university/work in the past year

Jokes or taunts of a sexual nature
37%

Seeing pictures or videos of girls or women that made them uncomfortable
26%

Seeing sexually explicit pictures or videos
25%

Unwanted sexual attention
20%

Unwanted touching
19%

Seeing rude or obscene graffiti about girls or women
18%

Sexual abuse on social media eg Twitter
15%

Frequent unwanted attention
14%

None of these
36%

Faced some form of sexual harrassment
59%

(21%), it does indicate that there is considerable interest in specific political topics. Girls and young women feel they don't receive adequate political education, which the majority say they would like. More than half of those aged 11 to 21 feel that politicians do not listen to the views of girls and young women enough (57%). Most girls agree that there are not enough female MPs (67% of 11- to 21-year-olds) and that girls' voices would be listened to more if there were more female MPs (63%). Over half also say that more diversity in Parliament would encourage them to be more interested in politics.

Girls are speaking out

The findings clearly show that girls and young women are getting a raw deal in many areas of their lives for many different reasons. But it's also clear that they can see how things could be improved for themselves and all young people.

They have put forward some of their own ideas for change, and identify who else they believe needs to take action – including educators, politicians and the government, and media organisations.

We can see that girls and young women are eager for change and that they see a place for themselves in making that happen. We all need to stand alongside them now and play a part in securing the rights and opportunities the next generation deserves.

Published in 2014

⇨ The above information is reprinted with kind permission from Girlguiding. Please visit www.girlguiding.org.uk for further information.

We ignore gender at our peril when creating a working future for young women

Trade unions have been at the forefront of fighting for women and men to be treated fairly and to avoid discrimination in the workplace.

By Carole Easton

As Chief Executive of a charity working with and on behalf of young women as they enter employment for the first time I wouldn't, of course, argue that this isn't anything but vital. Many of the young women I have spoken to have been exploited by employers, for example by being paid less than the National Minimum Wage.

But to achieve fairness and equality, different and tailored solutions are needed for men and women.

Women are over-represented in part-time and insecure jobs, four out of five of people stuck on low pay for more than ten years are women, caring responsibilities have a disproportionate impact on women and the pay gap is a long way from being closed.

In Young Women's Trust's new report, *Creating a Working Future for Young Women*, we call for a gender-specific response to the crisis of young women's worklessness.

The report is the result of a year-long inquiry into young women NEET (those not in education, employment or training). It highlights the fact that many more young women than young men – 428,000 compared to 310,000 – are NEET. They will be NEET for longer – three years compared to two – and the impact will be deeper, forcing many to endure a lifetime of poorly paid, insecure jobs and unemployment.

Successive governments have failed to alter the fact that over the last decade an average of more than 130,000 more women than men have been NEET.

Young women share some challenges with young men, such as very high levels of young unemployment in some localities. But they also have additional and often insurmountable challenges which prevent them furthering their education or entering work.

Creating a Working Future for Young Women contains a number of recommendations, some of which will benefit young men and young women who are NEET – such as creating many more apprenticeships which do not require formal entry criteria (usually five A*–C GCSEs) and simplifying the access to funding for Further Education at least until age 25 – while some will undoubtedly benefit young women more:

⇨ Training providers of information, advice and guidance to ensure they are encouraging and supporting young women towards a broader range of subjects and careers.

⇨ Extending the provision of free childcare so that young mothers can work and study.

⇨ Gathering more data about young people who are 'economically inactive', of which over two thirds are young women, and work closely with them to address the issues that are making it impossible for them to actively seek work.

These are complex problems that won't be fixed overnight but they can be addressed; just as long as we take gender into account. To do otherwise means that any attempts will continue to fail, and to fail young women.

25 March 2015

⇨ The above information is reprinted with kind permission from Touchstone. Please visit touchstoneblog.org.uk for further information.

are losing female talent by default. It's a wake-up call about checking against weak employment practices that cause such negative experiences for mums who want to work.

⇨ "It's time for employers to do some housekeeping in their organisations to make sure hidden problems and difficulties are surfaced and dealt with quickly to ensure they have both diverse and inclusive working environments.

⇨ "This will allow them to benefit from the added value women can contribute. At a time when the war for talent is hotting up, action is essential. It's nonsense for talent to be wasted and discrimination in pregnancy and maternity, whether intended or not, is an urgent area to be addressed."

Publication of this research marks the launch of the Commission's #worksforme awareness initiative to reduce pregnancy and maternity discrimination. The Commission is providing practical advice and information for women and employers on their rights and responsibilities, as well as a practical toolkit with a step-by-step guide for employers on managing pregnancy and maternity.

The #worksforme resources will help employers to understand what they must do when an employee is pregnant, on maternity leave or returning to work, and how to ensure they are creating an environment that works for everyone.

⇨ The above information is reprinted with kind permission from Equality and Human Rights Commission. Visit www. equalityhumanrights.com.

Stop period tax: "You try having a period without a tampon – then tell me what's essential"

Laura Coryton, 21, tells Radhika Sanghani why she's campaigning to remove the five per cent tax women pay on sanitary products and explains how such a levy contributes to period shame.

Periods have been taxed since 1973. It was then that we began paying 17.5 per cent tax on sanitary products such as tampons and pads because the Government deemed them "non-essential" items. After a lot of campaigning, that same 'period tax' was dropped to five per cent in 2001.

So, we're still paying it now, albeit at a lower rate.

Laura Coryton, a 21-year-old student at Goldsmiths University, has had enough. She's launched a campaign on Change.org to "Stop period tax. Period" and has already garnered more than 41,000 signatures (at the time of writing) in a matter of months.

The goal of her petition is to persuade George Osborne, the Chancellor of the Exchequer, to reduce the UK's "outdated, damaging" sanitary tax from five to zero per cent.

"It sends out a damaging message to society and says women aren't important, and that's a really dangerous message to send," Coryton tells me. "On principle it's a really damaging tax that really has no relevance in the 21st century.

"I think it's important to overturn mainly because of the original reason the tax was placed – which was because a really male dominated Parliament thought sanitary products weren't essential."

Although the levy is obviously a concern, a five per cent sanitary tax will only cost the average woman £3 a year out of an approximate £60 spend. It means Coryton's biggest issue is with the symbolism of the tax.

Period tax leads to period taboo

"I think it definitely supports [a societal] period taboo, that periods should be something we should be ashamed of and shouldn't talk to the male Parliament about. I think women have been made to feel shameful about menstruation for a very long time and I think the period taboo needs to be challenged and I think it has no relevance whatsoever. Having a period should be if anything something you celebrate because it shows you're in good health."

The idea that periods are "non-essential" particularly irks her – and the other 41,000 campaign supporters – especially as incontinence pads, exotic meats and edible sugar flowers are not taxed. "Sanitary products are just essential because without them periods would be fairly uncomfortable and we wouldn't be able to combat their physical consequences," she says.

"We understand there's a campaign for free bleeding [where women don't use any sanitary products] and staying at home, and that's absolutely fine but we're arguing people should have the choice."

An EU issue

It makes sense, but the difficulty with her request is that the decision lies with the European Union and not the UK Government. For an item to become exempt from tax, all 28 member states in the EU would have to agree. It's why the tax was only reduced to five per cent back in 2001 – it was the lowest possible option under EU law.

Several MPs have already told Coryton that her UK-based petition is a lost cause for exactly those reasons and that she'd be better off approaching the European Parliament directly. Kerry McCarthy, the Labour MP for Bristol East, even told Bristol Women's Voice: "Sadly it seems unlikely that the UK would be able to secure unanimous agreement [from the EU's member states], particularly as relations with other EU members are not good at the moment."

But Coryton thinks that this shouldn't be a reason to accept the current period tax. "So the reaction we have got from a lot of politicians has really annoyed me and made me feel even more passionate about the subject," she says. "They have said it will be difficult to eradicate so we shouldn't try."

She does have some MPs on her side, such as Labour's Stella Creasy, MP for Walthamstow, and Dawn Primarolo, MP for Bristol South who led the 2001 campaign to have the period tax reduced. Their plan is to wait till Parliament is back from its recess in September, and start rallying support so they can eventually raise the matter in the European Parliament.

Men support it too

The petition is already gaining a lot of support, something that Coryton didn't expect. She assumed that because the campaign has no real news hook ("it's essentially fighting against a 1973 law"), it would be hard for it to catch on. "I thought people have sort of just forgotten [about the issue]," she explains. "It's not something you think about."

She says the 2001 reduction was portrayed as a "small victory" so "people thought, oh OK it's only £3 a year, who really cares?"

"But now it's easy to rally people up with things like Change.org - it's just to remind people that it does matter and that it should be zero per cent. I just thought no one would really care because it's about periods. But then we attracted so many male supporters – which shouldn't be so surprising but is – as they can't really relate as much," she says excitedly.

It's not just a women's issue

Coryton originally billed the campaign as a women's issue, but after a comment from a transgender person who self-identified as a man but still menstruated, she realised that it shouldn't be described in such narrow terms.

"We have tried to avoid using words like this is a women's issue," she says. "It's not necessarily [just] a women's issue. Although it predominantly is, it's not exclusively that way."

The campaign has also received criticism from people who call her "another insecure mad feminist" and been trolled by others who suspect that she is against tax as a whole. But it's this latter jibe that frustrates her more than anti-feminist sentiment. "We're specifically not against tax," she stresses. "We are just against the ludicrous nature of tax allocation backed by George Osborne."

Which leads us back to her target Mr Osborne. This petition is directed at him, and Coryton wants him to listen closely: "He needs to update the tax allocations that he's backing as a Tory minister and to make a stand and say that 'this isn't how the Government feels – we don't think women are less important and that even if it's difficult, it's a tax worth fighting because sexism has no place whatsoever in our tax system'."

Now all that remains to be seen is whether Mr Osborne takes that message on board, and relays it to the European Parliament.

6 August 2014

⇨ The above information is reprinted with kind permission from *The Telegraph*. Please visit www.telegraph.co.uk for further information.

Key facts

⇨ In the UK, women gained the right to vote in 1928. However, it was not until 1979 that the world took concerted measures to end discrimination against women. That year, the UN passed a convention known as CEDAW: the Convention on the Elimination of All Forms of Discrimination against Women. (page 1)

⇨ 2013 saw a number of ground breaking episodes in the journey towards gender equality. One of the quirkier changes was the relaxation of French laws prohibiting women in Paris from wearing trousers. (page 1)

⇨ Some studies suggests that the expansion of the garment industry has also motivated many girls to stay in school. Around 80% of employees in the sector are female, and the jobs on offer require literacy, numeracy and cognitive skills. (page 2)

⇨ In the 1970s American psychologist Robert Brannon defined the four basic rules of masculinity as:

  • No sissy stuff – reject all that is associated with femininity

  • Be a big wheel – wealth, power and status define your success as a man

  • Be a sturdy oak – reliable and strong in a crisis

  • Give 'em hell – men are associated with risk, daring and aggression. (page 6)

⇨ Participants told the Government Equalities Office that while there is a mass of evidence about body image and sexualisation, it is not always robust and doesn't pay enough attention to issues such as gender, race or socio-economic status. (page 7)

⇨ Parents can now decide to share the Government allowance of 52 weeks maternity leave and 39 weeks of statutory pay. (page 11)

⇨ Ladybird, the iconic publisher of children's books including the classic Peter and Jane reading scheme, has vowed to remove any 'boy' or 'girl' labels from its books because it doesn't want "to be seen to be limiting children in any way". (page 15)

⇨ 20% of boys play on collaborative online games every day vs 2% of girls. (page 18)

⇨ Four times the number of boys as girls consider a career in engineering and computing. (page 18)

⇨ Only 27% of women on low pay say they always have enough money to cover their household living costs. (page 24)

⇨ Over one in five of the low paid women surveyed by Survation had degree-level qualifications. 37% of these women felt overqualified and over-skilled for their job, and among these one of the top three reasons given was caring for children. (page 25)

⇨ Two-parent families where only the father works have become a minority in many European countries and make up only around a fifth (22%) of families in the UK, according to analysis of data from the EU Labour Force Survey between 2001 and 2011. (page 26)

⇨ Of the eight countries looked at in the European Social Survey, UK fathers reported the highest levels of conflict between paid work and family life.

  • 35% of UK fathers said they always or often worry about work problems when not working; 17% said this never happens.

  • 37% of UK fathers said they are always or often too tired after work to enjoy the things they would like to do at home; 8% said this never happens. (page 26)

⇨ The usual working week of fathers working full-time in couple households has fallen from 47 to 45 hours per week. (page 26)

⇨ The Office for National Statistics reported in 2013 that the average age of all mothers had risen to 30 for the first time on record. (page 27)

⇨ Men who work part-time earn 5.4% less than part-time women on average, based on median hourly pay. However, the part-time gender pay gap varies with age. For part-time men, for example, the biggest gap occurs in 30–39 age group where the gender pay gap is 7.8%. (page 29)

⇨ On average women spend at least twice as much time on household work than men and four times as much time on childcare. (page 31)

⇨ Three in four girls aged 11 to 21 know girls their age who self-harm (76%) or suffer from depression (73%), and two in three know someone with an eating disorder (66%). (page 33)

⇨ Around four in five British women say being a mother is "more important" than having a career, while only 6% put having a career first. (page 36)

⇨ 10% of women are discouraged by their employer from attending antenatal appointments. (page 37)

⇨ 9% of women said that they were treated worse by their employer on their return to work than they were before pregnancy. (page 37)

⇨ Periods have been taxed since 1973. It was then that we began paying 17.5 per cent tax on sanitary products such as tampons and pads because the Government deemed them "non-essential" items. After a lot of campaigning, that same 'period tax' was dropped to five per cent in 2001. (page 38)

Equality Act 2010

This act brings a number of existing laws together in one place. It sets out the personal characteristics that are protected by law, and behaviour which is unlawful. The 'protected characteristics' are age; disability; gender reassignment; marriage and civil partnership; pregnancy and maternity; race; religion and belief; sex, and sexual orientation. Under the act people are not allowed to discriminate against, harass or victimise another person because they have any of the protected characteristics.

Feminism

Advocating women's rights and equality between the sexes.

Gender

Gender is sexual identity, especially in relation to society or culture; the condition of being female or male. Gender refers to socially-constructed roles, learned behaviours and expectations associated with females and males. Gender is more than just biology: it is the understanding we gain from society and those around us of what it means to be a girl/woman or a boy/man.

Gender quotas

A statement that an organisation or body must employ a minimum number of employees from a certain gender, in order to address a lack of male or female representation.

Gender stereotypes

Simplifying the roles, attributes and differences between males and females. Gender stereotyping encourages children to behave in ways that are considered most typical of their sex. For example, buying pink toys for girls and blue for boys, or limiting girls to playing with dolls and boys to toy-cars.

Glass ceiling

The term 'glass ceiling' refers to the problem of an invisible 'barrier' that prevents someone from progressing in their career to upper-level positions. Particularly for women and minorities.

HeForShe

A campaigned launched by UN Women and championed by actress Emma Watson. HeForShe aims to engage men in the fight for women's rights and gender equality.

Occupational segregation

Some kinds of jobs, occupations and sectors are dominated by men, and others by women. This is known as occupational segregation. For example, women may be more likely to work in the caring professions – nursing or childcare, for example – whereas men are more likely to work in manual labour. The undervaluing of what has traditionally been seen as 'women's work' is one of the reasons for the gender pay gap.

Pay gap

The gender pay gap refers to the difference between men and women's earnings. Currently, women earn on average 21% less than their male counterparts.

Period tax

Women currently pay a 5% tax on sanitary products because the Government does not consider them to be 'essential items'. A Change.org petition has been launched to try and have the tax removed. The main issue among campaigners is not the monetary value of the tax, but the principle that sanitary products are deemed non-essential.

Sex/gender discrimination

Treating someone differently because they are male, female or transgendered, resulting in a disadvantage to them in a certain area of life, e.g. employment, education.

Sexual abuse

Sexual abuse occurs when a victim is forced into a sexual act against their will, through violence or intimidation. This can include rape. Sexual abuse is always a crime, no matter what the relationship is between the victim and perpetrator.

Sexual bullying/harassment

This includes a range of behaviours such as sexualised name-calling and verbal abuse, mocking someone's sexual performance, ridiculing physical appearance, criticising sexual behaviour, spreading rumours about someone's sexuality or about sexual experiences they have had or not had, unwanted touching and physical assault. Sexual bullying is behaviour which is repeated over time and intends to victimise someone by using their gender, sexuality or sexual (in)experience to hurt them.

Assignments

Brainstorming

⇨ In small groups, discuss what you know about gender equality. Consider the following points:

- What does the term 'gender equality' mean?

- List as many things as you can think of that are 'unequal' between men and women.

Research

⇨ Read the article Girls' Attitudes Survey on page 33 and, in groups or as a class, create a questionnaire to distribute throughout your school that will investigate similar issues.

⇨ Choose a country other than your own and, using the Internet, do some research to find out about gender equality in that country. Write some notes on your findings and feedback to your class.

⇨ Using the tables on page 28 create a series of graphs to illustrate the data.

⇨ Visit a local bookshop and go to the children's section. Is there a clear divide between the books aimed at girls and the books aimed at boys? How can you tell if a book is aimed at boys rather than girls? Make some notes on your findings and share with your class.

Design

⇨ Design a poster that illustrates at least three gender equality issues faced by women in the UK.

⇨ Choose one of the articles in this book and create an illustration to highlight the key themes/message of your chosen article.

⇨ What is the difference between sex and gender? Create a diagram which could be used in a book for Key Stage 3 pupils, exploring this distinction.

Oral

⇨ "We shouldn't fight for 'gender equality'. We should fight to abolish gender," Debate this motion as a class, with one group arguing in favour and the other against.

⇨ Divide your class into two halves. One half should discuss male stereotypes and the other should discuss female stereotypes. Create a poster to demonstrate your ideas and then share with the rest of your class.

⇨ Research the HeForShe campaign and, in small groups, create a PowerPoint presentation that you could perform for your year group. Your presentation should aim to increase awareness of the HeForShe campaign and its goals.

⇨ As a class, discuss whether you believe men should be the primary 'breadwinners' of the household.

⇨ The character James Bond, from the film franchise and the novels by Ian Flemming, has always been written as male. However, there have recently been murmurings that the next James Bond character should be played by a woman. In small groups, discuss your reaction to this idea and list the different character traits of James Bond that you think would, or would not, work in a female lead.

⇨ 'Women in the West don't know how lucky they are. They complain of persecution while women in Saudi Arabia, for example, are denied such basic freedoms as the right to drive.' Do you think this is a fair statement? Discuss your views with a partner.

Reading/writing

⇨ Find out about the history of votes for women in the UK and write a blog post exploring your feelings around the issue.

⇨ Read Blurring gender lines in the toy aisle, on page 14 and write a summary for your school newspaper.

⇨ Imagine you work for a charity which campaigns for fathers' rights in the UK. Write a blog-post for your charity's website explaining the issues surrounding fathers' rights and why they are important.

⇨ Write a one-paragraph definition of gender equality.

⇨ Choose one of the illustrations from throughout this book and write 300 words exploring the themes the artist has chosen to depict.

⇨ Watch the 2003 film Mona Lisa Smile, starring Julia Roberts, and write a review exploring the role of women as portrayed by the director.

⇨ Imagine that you have voted 'for' the proposal that 'tampon tax' should be scrapped. Write a social media post in support of the Change.org petition. Your post should be at least 200 words and should aim to encourage others to empathise with your point of view.

⇨ Read the novel A Handmaid's Tale by Margaret Atwood, the story of a future dystopia in which women are virtually enslaved in accordance with an extreme interpretation of Old Testament morality. Write a review, focusing on how the book portrays notions of gender and identity through the character of Offred.

Acknowledgements

The publisher is grateful for permission to reproduce the material in this book. While every care has been taken to trace and acknowledge copyright, the publisher tenders its apology for any accidental infringement or where copyright has proved untraceable. The publisher would be pleased to come to a suitable arrangement in any such case with the rightful owner.

Images

All images courtesy of iStock, except page 39 © Cara Acred.

Icons on pages 7, 18, 24, 25 and 41 courtesy of Freepik.

Icons on page 31 courtesy of allsilhouettes.com

Illustrations

Don Hatcher: pages 8 & 22. Simon Kneebone: pages 14 & 37. Angelo Madrid: pages 4 & 35.

Additional acknowledgements

Editorial on behalf of Independence Educational Publishers by Cara Acred.

With thanks to the Independence team: Mary Chapman, Sandra Dennis, Christina Hughes, Jackie Staines and Jan Sunderland.

Cara Acred

Cambridge

January 2016